Julian Rose

Julian Rose was born in March 1947, on the Hardwick Estate in South Oxfordshire's Chiltern Hills, the youngest of four children to the heir of the thousand acre estate and baronetcy, passed down from his great grandfather.

On leaving school, Julian sought to harmonise strong artistic aspirations with the demands and responsibilities of his new found role as a 'landowner'.

Returning to the UK in 1967, he worked alongside his mother, developing the estate's farming and forestry enterprises. In 1969, he moved to London and won a place at the Royal Academy of Dramatic Art, going on to work in regional repertory theatres as an actor/stage manager.

He moved back to Hardwick in 1983, to become a full-time farmer, completing the conversion of the estate to organic farming methods, a process started in 1975, making him one of the pioneers of this ecological land management system. Joining the board of the Soil Association in 1984, Julian became involved in an intense campaign to promote ecological food and farming in the face of the rapid rise of industrial agriculture.

Julian also gained notoriety as both a defender and promoter of holistic approaches to the rejuvenation of struggling rural economies. Notably his unremitting insistence on the need to support local and regional, as opposed to 'global', food economies. An approach coined in a formula he named "The Proximity Principle". He sought to raise awareness of the need to build a dynamic balance between economic, social and environmental concerns. Never just one or the other.

In 1990, he took on the position of agricultural correspondent of the green broadsheet 'Environment Now', becoming one of the first UK activists to warn of the impending dangers of genetically modified foods.

In 2000 Julian was invited to become a co-director of the International Coalition to Protect the Polish Countryside, co-launching a highly successful 'Campaign for a GMO-Free Poland' as well as leading a high-profile defence of peasant farmers whom he holds up as the true guardians of biodiversity throughout the world.

He is the author of two acclaimed titles: *Creative Solutions to a World in Crisis: The Power of Locality* (2nd ed.) and *In Defence of Life*.

Overcoming the Robotic Mind
Why Humanity Must Come Through

Julian Rose

Dixi Books

Copyright © 2019 by Julian Rose
Copyright © 2019 Dixi Books
All rights reserved. No part of this book may be used or reproduced or transmitted to any form or by any means, electronic or mechanical, including photocopying, recording, or by any information and retrieval system, without written permission from the Publisher.

Overcoming the Robotic Mind - Why Humanity Must Come Through
Julian Rose
Editor: Assel Borambayeva
Designer: Pablo Ulyanov
Cover Design: Barbara Malina
Printed in Bulgaria
I. Edition: June 2019

Library of Congress Cataloging-in Publication Data
Julian Rose, 1947.
ISBN: 978-619-7458-47-3
1. Ecology 2. Adult Non-Fiction 3. Mind 4. Philosophy
5. Artificial Intelligence

© Dixi Books Publishing
46 Harrier Mews, SE28 0DQ London, UK
info@dixibooks.com
www.dixibooks.com

Overcoming the Robotic Mind
Why Humanity Must Come Through

Julian Rose

The Voice of the New Age

Contents

Preface	11
Humanity and Inhumanity	13
The hour is getting late	13
Why humanity must come through	17
Thinking: a criminal act	22
Us and them … or just us?	26
Life and Land	31
Sustainable agriculture and the European Union - are they compatible?	31
The battle to save the small farmers of Poland	37
Fake food versus real food - a question of life or death	41
The farmer is the future	45
Genetics	51
The war on human DNA. True humanity - or transhuman singularity and gene genocide?	51
From immaculate conception to genetic deception… leading to the rise of the crypto male	56

Man or Robot?   67

More on the transhumanist singularity   67
The anatomy of cyborg man
'Overcoming the Robotic Mind'   73
The re-engineering of life   78

Technology that Deceives   83

Smart phones and stupid people   83
Sedation by soundbite   88
Tweeting our way to oblivion   91

Raising the Spirit   97

The subjugation of the Creator   97
Concerning the integration of past experiences   101
The great turning   105
Seizing control of our destinies   108
The world is our garden   113

Politics of Deception   119

European superstate - one step closer or
imminent collapse?   119
The criminal duplicity of the mainstream journalist   126
At the point of no return   129
Sold a lie   133

Reassessing Religion   139

A Brief history of mind control: from the Christian
Cross to the mobile phone tower   139
Original sin - a myth whose time is up   145
Waiting for God   153
Organic hierarchy or dark side deception?   158

At War   **163**

The gender ending agenda...or the de-sexing of man and woman   163
The madness of war   171
Collectively realised creation versus mutually assured destruction   176
The global warming matrix   180
Ecocide or we decide?   183

Technocracy, Globalisation and Totalitarianism   **187**

Closing the gate on GMO and the criminal TTIP   187
Beyond a failing European superstate- deciding the future we want   193
On the faultlines of change: local versus global   199
The democratic experiment is finished   202
No time left - the dynamics of the new resistance   208

Becoming Conscious   **215**

A Great initiation called death   215
Healing the psychic split which causes war   220
Seven stumbling blocks on the road to consciousness   226
The power of NO   234
Echo of the primitive   237

Epilogue   **241**

Dialogue between a Master A and his Pupil B   241

Preface

The chapters of this book were assembled prior to the commencement of the public roll-out of 5G electromagnetic microwave telecommunication systems. The telecommunication's industry is doing this in defiance of the widespread publication by doctors and scientists, of 5G's potentially devastating affect on the health and welfare of people, animals, plants and insects.

5G telecommunications and WiFi, with its dual delivery system comprising ground situated base stations and space-based satellites, is designed to blanket the entire planet with invisible and highly invasive microwaves.

Completely untested for its health and safety implications, it represents the zenith of the technological megalomania dealt with at length in the pages of this book.

03/03/2019

Humanity and Inhumanity

The hour is getting late

There is a very real drama unfolding all around us, and also within each one of us. The intensity of this drama is without recent precedent and is now being realised on a stage spanning the length and breadth of the planet and beyond.

It's a race against time, played out within a gathering storm of conflicting energies. Human aspiration and inspiration clashing head-on with inhuman domination and destruction. And we are all caught in the gathering turbulence, witnessing the rapid dissolution of props and pillars we once took to be secure and dependable fixtures of our daily lives.

Our home, this planet, is in crisis; raped, polluted and torn by war, she is being pushed towards collapse— while the majority of human society carries on as though there were no crisis at all; just a number of disturbances, inconveniences and maybe a slightly unsettling feeling creeping in at the edges.

So long as the great majority experience life this way, the non-human forces of repression and destruction are winning the race. But so long as this predatory army is shrinking and the forces of aspiration and inspiration are advancing, the race is shifting in favour of victory for a great transformation in human awareness—accompanied by a healing of the third degree wounds suffered by this planet.

Where are you within this unfolding drama? Are you consciously channelling your energies in support of Life? Or are you still caught in the cul-de-sac of a stagnating status quo?

It has never been more crucial to know the answer to this question. It has never been more important to know what you're doing with your life, and to take action in making the shift so as to align with an emotional and actual commitment to working towards victory for the forces of creativity, imagination and joy.

Time is running out for anyone still sitting on the fence. I'll restate that slightly differently: time has run out for those still sitting on the fence.

Yes, every day that passes without one putting one's energy firmly behind the push for deep and lasting change for the better, is now going the other way: a contribution to that which is aligned with decline and death. Every day.

The hour is getting late. There is no 'middle ground' left. The four horses of the apocalypse can be heard making their long approach—but do not allow yourself to be mesmerised by the sound of their hooves. Turn instead to face their advance. Stand as strong as a pillar of oak in your resistance.

Let all fear be banished from your veins. Find in yourself that total resolution you know you have.

It was for times of great difficulty that you were gifted this power. Divine power.

Use it. It's the last chance. Abuse it—and that chance is blown. The Universe is awaiting your move, and time itself has come to a halt. Your response is attended upon by all the forces of creation. Yes, I'm talking to you.

Drop the old baggage right where you stand. There's nowhere left to go except where you have to go. If you try to stay in some in-between space, you're lost, because it doesn't exist. There is no space in between, except a virtual reality one. The world of lost souls, millions of them, clinging to that which is unreal; figments of an abstracted grasping mind, divorced from the true soul that would guide it on its way. The way.

Why cling to the illusory? It has nothing to offer you and you have nothing to offer it—it's a place of ghosts.

There is great danger on this planet, but it's not the kind of danger you're thinking about. It's the danger that you won't act when all that is energetic is calling upon you to act. Calling you to join the resistance against the forces of destruction. That is the greatest danger any individual can face; not acting when everything which actually matters is screaming for one to act.

I don't want to overdo the words, time is precious. I want to inspire your inner sun, not your powers of reasoning, however useful they may be. I want to feel you come alive with the power you are presently sitting on; sitting stewing on the reasons why you can't make the changes you know you have to make.

Everything else is moving on. This Universe is expanding, still hungry, still exploring, still adventuring.

Have you lost your appetite?

The dark side strategists feed on those who are not in movement. They proclaim the benefits and convenience of stagnation. They need their slaves. They maintain their energies by feeding on yours! And until you act, you are prostituting yourself to them. Every time you go to their kingdoms to buy your depleted food, pharmaceuticals and whatever constitutes the fashion of the day, you prostitute yourself to the world of consumption. The sterile, denatured world of the soulless materialist, that's killing off our inner joy and living planet. Yet you think it's all just normal! Or, you don't think at all.

Now you're getting a kick to wake up to the reality and to act on it. It's a rather bigger kick than usual, because now you're in the last chance saloon—and you've got no time left to sit around wondering what to do about it.

The hour is getting late, my friend.

The centrally controlled trading blocs of the world are tightening the noose. Those who preside over them are aiming for absolute control over all the resources of the planet; to own them. This means that even the vegetable seeds you might want to plant in your garden will be illegal unless you buy them from the trading bloc approved corporation. Genetically modified, for your convenient consumption.

Governments won't step in to save the situation, because governments are in the employ of corporations and not the other way around. They'll go to war and rip the skin right off the face of the planet to get what they want.

Your reaction to this should be "Not while I'm alive on this planet, they won't!" But instead it's more like:

"Oh God, what will stop them?" Or "Is it really that bad?"

You see, you're not being primed by outrage. 'Outrage' is the fire that drives one to take action, and if instead of outrage there's just a weak little flame flickering dimly in the dark, then you're going to get swept away, like the rest of them.

Prime your lamp right now, turn up the wick, feel the absurdity of a world where nobody bothers to do anything that matters, but instead devote themselves to everything that doesn't matter one iota! Get outraged by the sheer lunacy of this situation.

You are a child of creation—and yet you seem paralysed and unable to create.

Have you ever considered that you might be living someone else's life? That the person you see in the mirror is not actually you at all? No, it's the person you have tried to be, all this time—and that person is a mind-controlled being. A being who has been fed the pap propaganda of the status quo: a totalitarian agenda in the making.

That reflection in the mirror is an indoctrinated being who has suffered the fate of all those who fail to question the endless stream of deceptions which pour out of the control system that runs this planet.

When I warn you that you are walking blindly down a road to hell, you are more concerned about what the temperature will be when you get there—than on getting off that road, whatever the cost.

Yes, the hour is getting late. Most of your friends have no conception of this fact. They continually try to talk you out of having any such notions. They do not want you to jump ship and become your own master.

But I've said enough. Time to find the answers in yourself. Activate your survival mechanism; call forth the godly powers that will transport you to where you need to be. Do it: here and now.

Find your courage and never let go.

I'll meet you again on that road—or not at all.

Why humanity must come through

Need I say it, we are living in—and through—an apocalyptic time. Disintegration and destruction manifest themselves at an accelerating pace as our World is buffeted by a jumbled combination of opposing energies: the distorted man-made toxic ones as well as the universal vibratory waves that are an integral part of great cosmic changes.

Nothing we have experienced up until now quite compares with this. There is little that could prepare us for our journey through this collision of forces, aside from an emerging awareness that they are both external and internal manifestations. Manifestations of human and universal energies seeking to redefine and rebalance their shared essence.

Consider for a moment the contribution that our own specifically 'man-made' toxic cocktail makes to this confusion. Here's just a few: electromagnetic smog; atmospheric aerosol pollutants; weather engineering; leaking radioactivity from nuclear power plants; a continually active war machine; blanket agrichemical pesticide contamination of both air and soil; transgenic crops and animals; nanotech foods, oil spills or leaks; chemically assisted fracking for gas; pharmaceutical and industrial pollution of air, water and food; and—not least—the deliberate distortion of human energies via materialistically loaded propaganda, and its mindless being splashed about by unquestioning followers of a moribund status quo.

The extremity of this multi-pronged violence enacted upon our living planet, its peoples, plants and animals, has led to the suggestion that humanity will pay the ultimate price and be wiped out. Destroyed by its own hand; its own uncontrolled hubris. Its failure to overcome its own shortcomings.

Some say the planet, battered and bruised as it is, will be better off without man.

That freed from its chief oppressor, Gaia will more assuredly survive and heal; will find her equilibrium anew and come through—restored.

It is quite easy to sympathise with this view, not least because it seems to provide an answer to those who feel closer to nature than to their fellow humans, and can see no redemption for a mankind so determinedly set on the path of self-destruction.

Yet, even when taking into account the tragic mismanagement of humanity's journey thus far, I do not consider this to be any kind of answer. For, it is my contention, with man out of the picture, the advancement of universal equilibrium—however erratic—will be completely arrested. On the macrocosmic level, I believe a world without human beings would constitute a major setback for the entire universe. And at the microcosmic level, a major setback for the plant, animal and insect kingdom as well.

Why do I say this?

Imagine for a moment the vast arena we call the cosmos. It is a vibrant intelligent life force. Intelligent, because it is at once self-governing and on the move. It is in a state of permanent transition——never static. As it expands (and it still is expanding) it discovers itself ... just as we discover 'ourselves' as we gain awareness and experience. We share with the cosmos a common intelligence which is without limitation, except in as much as it is held in check by counterproductive forces of entropy.

So humanity draws down unto itself the intelligence which is manifest in all elements of the cosmos. While standing behind that cosmic intelligence—and informing it—is the omnipotent, omnipresent source of Supreme Consciousness; a characteristic of which is infinite creativity and unquenchable curiosity.

The intelligent cosmos is an expression of Supreme Consciousness's natural exigency. But the Supreme Consciousness cannot experience who or what He/She/It is until those exigencies solidify and take on form; offering a reflection of that which goes into them.

How do we know this?

Because it is in us that these Source based exigencies take on earthly expression. We are the earthly torch bearers of the Divine spark. It is in us that those Divine exigencies take form. And to the degree to which we earthbound beings in turn start sending back to the intelligent cosmos our own exigencies—expressed as love, joy, pleasure, pain—so Source gains greater or lesser degrees of awareness concerning (His) creation.

In us, Source sees a third density reflection of His divine exigencies! But not in us alone, of course. In every living being as well as rock, tree and sea—as they are all expressions of that One Supreme Consciousness.

However, out of the great diversity of beings and matter that compose our planet, man has emerged as the best equipped to consciously recognise in himself that infinite exigency which has its source in the Supreme Consciousness, God. Not only to recognise it, but to respond intentionally to its call: that pull we call 'aspiration'. That wonderful upwardly reaching joyous impulse which is the inherent birthright of all humanity.

Were this force to be wiped off the face of the planet—a great vacuum would be left in its place. For the plant and animal kingdoms cannot 'consciously' respond to the call of the intelligent cosmos, they can only act as reflexive recipients of its energies and act as mirror-like retransmitters. Yet we see and experience in plants and animals a special kind of purity—because they are uncorrupted reflections of divine intelligence—and in this way, a permanent source of inspiration to homo sapiens.

The plant and animal kingdoms do not have the free will and the evolved powers of self-determination that humanity possesses. So should humanity be destroyed—or destroy itself—the plant and animal kingdoms would lose their stepping stones towards acquiring states of self-determination and consciousness. Homo Sapiens represents this stepping stone, the next rung up the ladder of cosmic consciousness for the animal and plant kingdoms.

The fact that the great majority of mankind has so far failed to exercise its potential of cosmic consciousness is not a valid reason to conclude that it should be nullified.

We humans provide a link between the Supreme Consciousness and all other living and animated features of Gaia. It is just a small minority who set out to deliberately distort that link—and set themselves up in its place as the false gods of engineered hubris.

In our undistorted state, we are pulling on an invisible rope to which all living beings are attached. Next in line may be the dog which develops a strong affinity with its loving master/mistress. Maybe it will have the chance to return to Earth as a human in the next spirit cycle. The courageous cat or the sensitised horse likewise, and so on along the chain. Even rocks will eventually get their transformation chance. But, critically, only as long as all of life retains its spiral of forward and upward momentum, which it can only do if we humans fulfil our role in contributing our dynamic to that movement.

Everything on that jostling, energetic chain of life is aspiring towards becoming an ever more subtle form of itself. We included. Yet as the evolutionary energies move ever onwards—and not simply in a repeating circle—that Source, from which we all come—is itself also further evolving. What we yearn to 'return to' is itself in movement, continuously evolving and metamorphosing. However, its omniscient essence is retained throughout and will be instantly recognised as 'home'.

We humans occupy a pivotal point in all this. One which draws upon that which is below and aspires to that which is beyond. This places man in a unique position of responsibility towards the evolution of both Earth and Universe.

We humans have inherited powers that, when used wisely and creatively, can positively determine the future direction of Life both on the microcosmic and macrocosmic levels. And that equally, when used unwisely and destructively, can retard that same evolution. That is our gift from the Divine. We are entrusted with responsibility for this planet—and ultimately the entirety of universal evolution.

We are even gifted with the potential to influence the ongoing composition of that which our Creator imagined into existence. The Creator does not cling to power as delusional power-obsessed dictators do—but passes on the gift through us.

Therefore, should humanity be erased off the face of this Earth who will carry on the great experiment?

We are the ones to whom the baton of life has been passed and in whose hands its future rests. We are awaking to the realisation that 'to be human' means to occupy a pivotal role in furthering the work of Creation. That is a gift which surpasses all other blessings with which we are endowed.

So precious is it that we cannot but totally commit ourselves to and fully embrace our calling. And that means fully embracing the inclusivity of planetary diversity as expressed through all its multifarious species—the poverty or richness of whose lives is inseparably linked with the poverty or richness of our lives, and whether we are able or unable to fulfil the quest to realise that potential with which we are all endowed.

So for the sake of that which we call Creation, mankind must come through. Humanity must prevail.

Thinking: a criminal act

"If my thought-dreams could be seen, they'd put my head under a guillotine..."
(Bob Dylan)

Well Bob, I've got news for you—they can—and that is what lies in store for all of us unless the 'thought police' fail to get their newly evolved 'anti-humanity' mind scanning weapons legally integrated into everyday life.

As 'the war on terror' is notched up to a further level of intensity, and the false-flag flagellations of New World Order exponents start outnumbering the real flag emblems of nation states, we know that we are witnessing a serious expansion of the central control system's morbid attempt to dominate humanity and crush the power of independent thought and action.

Have no doubt, this is the intention. The current ongoing shepherding of great swaths of human beings into psychological pens of fear and passivity, is the precursor of a time in which any independent thought process will be treated as a serious threat to the 'normality' of a subdued and static status quo.

A 'thought crime' might include 'envisioning a better world' and considering ways of bringing it about.

But hold on ... aren't we here already? Those who challenge the status quo's perpetual commitment to war, resource mismanagement and rabid social inequality, are already seen as a threat to the state and singled out as potential terrorists.

It is only a small step from here to governments backing early warning counter-terrorist security measures that would legalise the brain scanning (overt and covert) of 'suspects' held to be harbouring illicit thoughts. As such thoughts, the argument would go, would be deemed to be forerunners to inciting antisocial and criminal behaviour.

Thus, to implicate the offender as a threat to the establishment, all that is needed is evidence that certain neurons situated in the area of the neocortex associated with 'free thinking', were actively engaged over 'x' period of time, and that this was sufficiently 'abnormal' for the individual to be singled out for special attention.

Under the designation 'Remote Neural Monitoring' we can already have our brains scanned and not even know it.

Yet the legacy of a largely brain-dead humanity is already strongly in evidence, and independently thinking individuals are an unusual enough commodity to be considered 'rare breeds', marginalised and even castigated, in this bleak era of fear induced mass conformism and mind-numbing political correctness.

We who follow our hearts and deeper intuitions do indeed belong in the rare breeds stable, and every attempt is being made to ensure that the stable door is locked and bolted so that we can no longer pass our messages to the outside world.

On the flip side of the same coin we have 'thought control'— which is at an advanced stage—having been a major part of the control system's sinister arsenal for many decades. A weapon with a special place in the carefully orchestrated strategy that surrounds the ever expanding 'war on terror'.

The Charlie Hebdo horror debacle in Paris serves as a powerful reminder of just how easily millions can be instantly brought into line when their everyday slavery is threatened by a sporadic act of preordained violence.

Let us briefly recount this phenomenon: a satirical magazine in Paris publishes, not for the first time, an insulting depiction of Mohammed. Right on cue, a clique of highly trained 'Muslim terrorists' occupy the magazine's HQ, killing members of the staff. The building is surrounded and the invaders are shot.

The violence, being vivid, open and rebellious, is depicted by mainstream media headlines, statesmen and the thought police, as a preposterous threat to the sanctity of freedom of speech and very fabric of French society. Tens of thousands of placards bearing the words "Je suis Charlie" are instantly rolled out, and the largest number of French citizens since the liberation of Paris at the end of World War II—well over 1.5 million—solemnly take to the streets holding up these placards "Je suis Charlie." And what really is this statement saying?

It is a show of solidarity with a sick periodical that deliberately inflames racist passions by pushing the legal parameters of freedom of speech to their limits, deliberately stimulating controversy and thereby attracting 'scandal value' sales. It is a political tool to incite hatred and racial prejudice.

Meanwhile the perpetrators of the killings are held up as symbols of Western hating Middle Eastern/Muslim sects, bent on dispensing carnage and death to a civilised, humanitarian, law-abiding Western nation. All of which is one huge deception—from beginning to end.

Outstanding for its outlandish hypocrisy is the extraordinary omission of the hell that has been unleashed, year-in year-out, on the peoples of Iraq, Libya, Afghanistan, Syria, by a carefully crafted US/UK/France military consortium. Those who masterminded the post-9/11 secret service sponsored vilification and destruction of anything that dared stand up to the hegemonic perpetual war ambitions of nations bereft of any vestige of humanitarian, spiritual or self-respecting values.

If the Charlie Hebdo attack had indeed been carried out, of their own free will, by those downtrodden and abused citizens of countries bombed to hell and back by US, UK and French invaders, the millions who took to the streets of Paris would be none the wiser. Their herd-like narcissistic response had already been assured.

They had been successfully mind-controlled into seeing

only that their freedoms and cultural mores had suffered an 'unprovoked' challenge.

This is the sedation formula which has been used in every one of the so called 'terrorist attacks' fomented and staged by the CIA, MI5 and Mossad triumvirate over the last two decades—and well before. Attacks that enabled posturing public figureheads to pronounce an indefinite 'war on terror'—the terror which they had themselves been instrumental in setting in motion.

Mind and thought control leads on directly to internet control. Charlie Hebdo film footage that showed contradictory evidence to the mainstream story, got taken down after more than 2 million hits in less than 24 hours—and there was no 'blood and gore' on the show—no excuse for the complete removal of this evidence. Since then, moves to control the internet have gathered pace.

All of us who run websites seeking to expose the lies and reveal the truth, know just how tenuous the situation is. Shots keep being fired across the bows of our information ships—and increasingly into them. It's been going on for years. But now, as the battle lines of extremism are once again been drawn and the orchestrated warmongering drum-rolls intensified, the glimmering lights of truth are systematically being shut down.

The 'solution' requires little speculation: a complete clampdown on any and all information that contradicts the controlling establishment's 'terrorist inspired' battle plan "all in the interests of public safety and long-term security", of course.

We can all play our part in countering this worldwide attempt to suffocate the voice of truth and reason and to replace it with a global ministry of lies. By resolutely refusing to be corralled into the grey soup of mass indoctrination we will be boldly flying the flag for the liberation of humanity.

It has come down to this. Holding our ground, thinking creatively and keeping open the lines of communication: these are now the primary tools of the resistance. The lines in the sand that we will never allow ourselves to retreat from.

It is from such acts of bravery that victory can and will be realised.

Us and them... or just us?

Is it possible that a thread of unity ties together even the most disparate of forces? Are we actually that different from those whom we think are our mortal enemies?

Is it possible that all humanity shares one collective unconscious?

These are important questions, because the old weapon of 'divide and conquer' is exercising an almost total paralysis over society at this time. Nothing new, you might say, but the remorseless sowing of the seeds of division has once again become a key weapon in whipping up factions to accept 'war' as the only, and inevitable, end point.

But this war-cry can only work if and when we fall prey to the corrosive indoctrination which accompanies the rhetoric of 'us and them'. Wars would not happen if the fuel for vindictive finger-pointing was no longer so easily assimilated into our everyday lives.

Now some might say that what's going on now is beyond such logic—that it's a totally other dimension of insanity that's driving the apocalyptic state of affairs on this planet. That can be a persuasive argument. However, it would be most unwise to leave ourselves out of the picture, as though we were mere observers and not players. For all that happens 'out there' has its seed in something that happens 'in here'. Events could and would be different if we could learn to recognise the symptoms of division both within ourselves and in our interactions with others.

So how do we best get a handle on this seemingly pervasive human weakness for 'us and them' which appears so open to exploitation by those who prosper from inciting faction and discord? The first response which I try to turn to when feeling irritably vulnerable to accusing someone of having wronged me, is what the French call 'mettre en place'—put yourself in the other's place. If one can master this technique, it gives the opportunity to have a look at what we are about to do or say, as though we ourselves were at the receiving end of it.

Now, when one gets a dose of one's own accusatory medicine it can have a quite dramatic effect!

"Oops, better not launch into that one, it's bound to provoke an equal or likely even stronger reaction." A reaction likely to be based more on defensiveness or anger than on reasoned argument based upon true feelings.

For a 'reasoned argument based on true feelings' should be the goal of all dialogue, of all intercourse. And if it were, we wouldn't have war. Because war starts with, and in, us. Our war state is unavoidable so long as we remain divided against ourselves. So long as the way we interact with others is clouded by egotistical and selfish concerns, rather than illuminated by reasoned and considered responses.

Now, a 'reasoned' response demands a pause.

A reflective moment or two to take in just exactly what it is that's going on. And in the space created by that reflective pause, we are able to reorder our emotional self. We are able to catch the moment and slow things down. Take a look in the mirror. Or stand in the shoes of the other party and consider just what we look/sound like to them.

Nine times out of ten, neither the accuser nor the accused has reflected for even one moment on what is driving the emotional exchange. So unless one of the participants (and ideally both) can step back and establish this reflective space—this non-partisan territory—then all too often things run quickly out of control. A blood rush leads to an irrational tit for tat exchange, which in turn creates further disharmony and a lingering sense of suspicion. This suspicion in turn becomes a fecund breeding ground for differences to grow hardwired and seemingly irreconcilable.

Irreconcilable difference is a stone's throw away from a state of war.

We know our world is teetering on the brink of major conflict. We feel disempowered by the sheer scale of the engineered divisions that stand behind this dire state of affairs. It is not an easy predicament for any of us to cope with. Yet the source of the insanity that is so readily on display on the global stage is not a far cry from that listless state of irritation and edginess which manifests itself within all of us when we feel cornered or unreasonably provoked.

How can we respond to the threat of war when we have not yet come to grips with our own unconscious reactionary responses within our day to day life concerns—let alone when faced with the irascible volatility of a planet on the edge of global conflict?

That 'pause' which I recommended in order to set our house in order, is the key. It's a technique employed by the most seasoned diplomats when faced with the need to diffuse and temper potentially dangerous accusation and aggression. But to deal with the world scale madness of today, such defusing skill needs to be magnified, deepened and made manifest as an expression of profound intent. Intent to uncover lies and falsity and to manifest truth, whatever the cost. For this is the only genuine antidote to the slippery slide into chaos.

Truth emerges out of inner peace. But such 'peace' is by no means passive; it is burning with conviction, determination and a rock-hard steadfastness of intent. The will to bring this world through—however badly scarred—and bring it to life once again, like the smile that lights up and transforms a baby's once forlorn face.

Why else are we here, if not to achieve mission impossible?

There is a collective unconscious. It is (slowly and quickly) awakening and transforming into a collective consciousness. It is happening mostly on unseen levels, yet it can be felt. Anyone can feel it, but not everyone will. That is because it is a seriously inconvenient truth for those whose wills are obdurately directed elsewhere. Towards the absolute denial of their reason to be; and then towards the annihilation of that which attempts to remind them.

Yet screaming murder at others will do nothing to ameliorate their fate or ours. For so long as we remain caught in a world of 'us and them' we are unable to achieve the breadth of vision which enables us to see beyond our bit part roles as 'antagonist' or 'victim' on this fretted stage of man-made conflict.

In the end, we all play our part in hastening the madness of war, unless or until we can dissolve the imaginary, deeply toxic dividing lines that set man against man, country against country, belief against belief.

The division lines are actually an illusion. An illusion made to feel real by the fear and falsity that serves to build up brittle walls of concrete—instead of dissolving into flowing rivers of empathy. It is division and conflict that provides fuel for the false gods and divisive demons that prey on the war fear of ordinary mortals. They would starve and fade away should that which feeds them finally be vanquished and consigned to the annals of history.

At this time of unmitigated warmongering and provocation, it's vital that we redouble our efforts to come together, both internally and externally, so as to expose that which feeds on the cancer of 'divide and conquer'—on the falsity of 'us and them'.

Those crazed forces that are willing to terminate life on Earth, just for the sake of an insatiable ego.

Let's remember that we are not actually hermetically sealed from that which appears to be inexorably alien to our beliefs and emotions.

For in the end, there is no us and them. There is only us.

Life and Land

Sustainable agriculture and the European Union - are they compatible?

If the agricultural policy of the European Union ever had any positive attributes—and this is questionable— they have long since been subsumed in a sea of bureaucracy. Worse than this, however, are the decisions emanating from the European Commission which this bureaucracy is supposed to enforce.

Let us remind ourselves that the European Commission is run by unelected technocrats, who have, over the years, granted themselves very substantial powers. Powers that carry with them the right to accept or reject vital policy decisions that affect us all every day of our lives. In the meantime, the European Parliament, which is an elected body, is largely consigned to the side lines, failing (more often than not) to imprint its conclusions on the statutory agenda overseen by the Commission.

So it is within this disturbingly autocratic context that we struggle to make an impression in our attempts to reform the Common Agricultural Policy and get taxpayers' money diverted to support those arenas that really need and merit it: the health and diversity of the food we eat, the countryside we love and those caring farmers who are the ultimate trustees of the land and all it produces.

Make no mistake, at present your money and mine is supporting a regime wholly antithetical to this wish list. With 80% of CAP funds going to just 20% of farms, something looks decidedly wrong. But when one becomes aware that the 20% of farms getting the cream are mostly large scale, monocultural factory farming units and agro-industrial commodity dealers, it becomes abundantly clear that the CAP is little more than an institutionalised banking arm of the corporate agribusiness cartel. A cartel that fields hundreds of 'lobbyists' to infiltrate the Brussels networks and ensure that EU Commissioners are wined, dined and made thoroughly replete with all the necessary propaganda to convince them of the merits of Big Pharma and its GMO and seed industry cousins.

Now, anyone with a sense of fairness and justice will immediately recognise that this is a grossly biased way of doing business. What small or even medium-sized business enterprise can afford to pay dozens of lobbyists to promote their cause? The 20% of our money, a small percentage of which is being made available to the millions of smaller farms that struggle to make a living, does not begin to address their needs if they are to survive and thrive in the cut-throat marketplaces of today's world.

Amongst such farms are virtually all the ecologically managed concerns, barring the few 'landed' large scale units, and the vast plethora of mixed traditional farming practices whose environment friendly methods have been passed down from generation to generation over centuries. These are the farms with whom the majority of the discerning public have the most sympathy—and with good reason. They produce the only food fit to eat in Europe (and beyond) today.

It is corporate agribusiness, in Europe as much as in the USA, which has made our money turning pristine meadows into monocultural deserts, that gets the lion's share of government and EU support. This leads to our hard-won tax payer contributions being used to trash the food chain and ensure that nitrate-soaked, sterile soils remain the foundation of the modern food chain. It also ensures the survival of the "efficiency and progress" dogma so beloved of politicians, academics and rapacious corporations. Such enterprises, after all, produce just about enough taxable revenue to convince bureaucrats that they are worth subsidising; whereas the majority of humane small and medium-sized family farms are operating at close to the poverty line, thereby failing to enrich government coffers. Their owners do at least retain their independence, preferring the time-honored farming 'way of life' to becoming slaves to global agribusiness.

EU subsidies are paid to farmers on a per hectare basis; so as long as this lasts, the largest farms will always get the greatest financial reward. In the USA there is a different route whereby big farming is subsidised, but it amounts to the same thing in the end. And so long as decision makers are locked into/up inside mainstream economic dictates that cannot see beyond the 'growth economy'—regardless of the fact that it destroys virtually all it touches—we will be hard pressed to save our planet from certain sickness and ultimate sterility.

Over the past three to four decades Europe and the US have experienced a rapid decline in agricultural land and number of small farms. Between 1960 and 2008, the EU lost 18% of its agricultural land and the same period has seen an intensification of agricultural practices concentrating on a smaller and smaller number of ever bigger farms. At the same time prices and rents have risen, severely restricting the opportunities for new applicants to enter the profession. At the same time those farmers who have been able to maintain their enterprises are financially squeezed by the relentless speculative fluctuations of the market and by rising farm costs that rarely match incoming revenue.

Additionally, all across Europe thousands of small community-scale processing plants and abattoirs have been driven out of business by having totally unrealistic and unaffordable EU 'sanitary and hygiene' regulations imposed upon them. This has caused the fragmentation and destruction of the entire infrastructure upon which quality food processors and farmers rely.

Could this mark the nadir of the CAP and the turning point for a radically reformed EU?

Clearly only a major shift in thinking can bring about the deeply rooted reforms that are needed to dig European agriculture out the ever deeper hole it finds itself pushed into.

The EU should start afresh by taking as its main point of emphasis 'Food Security and Food Sovereignty'. Each member state should be encouraged to draw up and implement plans to ensure that as many of its citizens as possible have direct access to adequate amounts of good quality, home grown, pesticide and GMO-free foods. As oil prices continue to fluctuate and targets to prevent further fossil fuel emissions are tightened and enshrined in legal acts, the mass transportation of foods across the world is clearly becoming a no go solution. Aside from wars, transportation has been identified as contributing the highest levels of toxic CO_2 emissions in our society and considerable environmental degradation.

EU and US policy makers should now be aware that rural economies do not thrive on the World Trade Organisation's global import/export model. Under the WTO regime money is sucked out of local communities and ends up in the ever-swelling pockets of vast supermarket chains that profit from a purchasing policy which coerces farmers into supplying mass produced commodities at knockdown prices. The upshot of this is a catalogue of farm bankruptcies, degraded environments, increasingly sterile devitaminised foods and a major public health crisis.

The EU has to part company with the WTO's Codex Alimentarus if it is to affect a realisable Food Security program in Europe.

Under current WTO rulings, the pressures to mass produce tailor-made 'cheap food' for a global market place are so great that farmers will extract the last ounce of fertility from the soil in an effort to fulfil their contractual obligations to the super and hypermarket chains that epitomise globalised food retailing. Agrichemical inputs, antibiotics, growth promoters, animal cloning, hydroponics, irradiation and even nanotechnology are now being turned to as ways of maintaining the mass production of foods to fulfil the market's rapacious demands. Thus once prolific rotational, bio-diverse farming practices carried out by generations of families who cared for the land, their farm animals and crops, are replaced by factory farming units that tick none of the boxes increasingly recognised as constituting good practice and 'sustainable' agriculture.

Under a regime redirected towards food security, the emphasis is not on import/export markets of mass produced commodities, but on stimulating self-sustaining local and regional supply and demand chains and the least environmentally destructive practices. Food 'quality' replacing food 'quantity' as the key focus, with new links forged between consumers and producers which greatly shorten the supply chain. This has the benefit of ensuring that fresh food is eaten in its optimum condition and as close as possible to its area of production—following a formula which I have called "The Proximity Principle".

The EU, and indeed all 'trading blocs' on this planet, should redirect their policies towards enabling and encouraging farmers and local authorities to establish strong circular regional food production and processing enterprises. Enterprises that catalyse the rural economies of the regions and lead to an abundance of distinctive, ecologically raised foods and that can be purchased directly off the farm, in local market places and in small to medium-sized retail outlets that offer 'local foods for local people'.

Food Security is also dependent upon high quality, vigorous seeds being widely available to farmers and growers. Therefore local 'living seed banks' should be strongly encouraged in order to fulfil this need. Non hybrid, traditional, non-engineered seeds have been shown to have greater vigour and more natural resilience than their finely tuned laboratory bred counterparts, when confronted by climactic fluctuations and air-borne disease.

The denaturing, patenting and corporate-monopolising of seeds via genetic engineering have no place in any serious plan to address and stimulate national and regional food security. GM cross contamination of neighbouring crops by wind-blown pollen, bees, insects, birds and people makes it impossible to establish an ecologically stable food chain. What is needed is the local and interregional biological integrity which gives citizens the confidence to purchase foods raised on land free from the toxic residues and the novel genotypes that form the basis of genetic engineering techniques.

It has been repeatedly shown that some 75% of Europeans don't want GM food products on their plates or in their fields. Such resistance has been vindicated by recent independent laboratory research studies carried out in four different European Countries, which have conclusively shown that rodents fed on a diluted GM feed diet suffered severe lesions of the liver as well as malfunctioning of the kidneys within one year. After two years the rodents became infertile and died. This provides an indication of what might happen to humans. It is only criminal negligence that has prevented GM crops being banned already.

The CAP (Common Agricultural Policy) exists because we pay for it. Almost no reasonably discerning citizen today actually wants his or her health to be compromised by the way in which our food is grown. We also don't want our countryside to be dominated by vast expanses of chemically forced crops whose nutritional quality is as poor as the sterile soils from which they come. Neither do we want animal concentration camps where thousands of chickens and pigs spend their suffocatingly short lives confined to airless, neon lit sheds and a diet of antibiotic laced GM soya and maize whose residues have been shown to contaminate our food supply.

An ever-growing number of EU citizens want real food from real farms and they want assurances that the methods used on these farms will not compromise their health or the health of the land the produce comes from. EU agricultural commissioner Dracian Coilos was one of the very few commissioners for agriculture who reflected these concerns in his pronouncements on CAP reform. He was doing so at the behest of a coordinated citizens' action movement pressing for a fundamental rethink of EU agricultural policies, bringing them in line with recommendations made by the 400 specialists and scientists who made up the IAASTD report of 2006. Namely: that traditional mixed family farms and biological farming methods are best able to ensure national food security, and that genetically modified foods will not be effective in ensuring an end to global hunger.

Consensus on this message has not been achieved; but is essential if European food and farming is to survive and thrive in the 21st century.

The battle to save the small farmers of Poland

I am writing this in the Polish Parliament in Warsaw (The Sejm). Jadwiga Lopata, founder of The International Coalition to Protect the Polish Countryside, myself (ICPPC President) and farmer colleagues from different regions of Poland, are in the parliament as part of a campaign we have been fighting for the past three years, to get the food laws changed. We are supported in this by a number of active consumers and, perhaps surprisingly, by the chairman of the Agricultural Committee, who belongs to the Kukiz 15 social movement which achieved 12% of the vote in the last election.

The current law in Poland discriminates heavily against the small and medium-sized traditional family farmers by prohibiting the on-farm processing of their traditional high quality foods. Also banning the sale of such foods in shops and other local and regional outlets.

The only way farmers can be on the right side of the law, is if they register themselves as 'a business' and carry out their processing activities in a separate building designed to satisfy 'hygiene and sanitary' regulations of the European Union and national government. Regulations that have been designed by supermarkets and the food industry for supermarkets and the food industry.

It's a stitch-up. A stitch-up that exists throughout the corporate dominated world of uniform, centralised, commercial food production and distribution.

But in Poland, the discrimination against 'real farmers' and 'real food' is particularly harsh; maybe because there are still around one million productive small and medium-sized farmers whose independent way of life presents a diametrically opposed position to that of agribusiness and Big Pharma. And it is because agribusiness and Big Pharma maintain a massive lobbying presence in Brussels, as well as at member state parliamentary levels, that EU officials and national governments nearly always toe the line which is sold to them by the lobbyists. Only highly energetic resistance stands any chance of breaking through this deeply biased charade.

We belong to this highly energetic resistance; and small as it is, we are making waves that increasingly cannot be ignored by the powers that be.

Already, back in 2006, we were able to enlist all sixteen Polish provinces into self-declaring themselves as 'GMO Free Zones', which led in turn to the government of that time introducing a total ban on the import and planting of GM crops and seeds. The first Country to do so in the Western World.

But the essentially devious nature of the ever changing—and never changing—political system, demands constant eyes-wideopen pressure in order for the voice of the people to be given any chance of enduring. In this case, small farmers, struggling to maintain their deeply endangered way of life.

In Poland's long history of foreign occupation (known as the partitions) peasant farmers played a vital role in the resistance. Their stubborn refusal to give up their land during the communist land nationalisation movement of the 1950's, caused the Russian military to give up their attempted colonisation of much of the Polish countryside.

It was acts of bravery like this, as well as the heroic Warsaw resistance movement of World War II, that endeared me to this nation. It inspired me to come to Poland to work alongside the repressed and often stigmatised peasant farmers whose love of the land and unassuming acceptance of a life of subsistence struck me as an enduring template for the future of this planet.

Yet these farmers, who once expressed defiance in the face of the attempted foreign take-over five decades ago, are now treated as criminals by their own government; their fine farmhouse foods being declared as 'illegal' while the sterile, denatured and tasteless supermarket foods are given the all-clear. What a shocking misappropriation of justice.

Rows of gentlemen (sic) in dark suits are sitting behind a long table in the consultation room. They are parliamentarians, who between them are highly unlikely to have any practical experience or understanding of the way of life of the small family farmer whose fate is largely in their hands. They represent mostly the 'no change' advocates of a sterilised status quo.

But there is also a ragamatag bunch of well-informed farmers and consumers raising their voices in support of a simpler, fairer, more just and honest approach than that of the cut-throat world of mass production and manipulated market places. An approach that would wrest power away from the corporate oppressors and open, once again, links to local communities as well as cooperative working and sharing practices.

Countryside bread makers, artisan cheese specialists, dairy farmers, bee keepers, fine sausage and ham makers, fruit and vegetable growers and many more—are, in reality, cultivators of the only real foods available to a public increasingly sold out to the Tescos, Carrefours and Lidls of this world. The KFC, McDonald's and Coca Cola infested urban junk food markets that are surreptitiously poisoning the population of this planet, and in the process turning human beings into pacified tools of the state.

Yet, only around twenty years ago, many communities throughout Poland were able to access their daily nutritional requirements direct from the farmer. And it is exactly that line, 'direct from the farmer', that we chose to spearhead our present campaign. Here is where we must be once more, because local, fresh flavourful artisan foods are a fundamental antidote to the 'legal', lifeless, carcinogenic, obesity promoting products that symbolise a world sliding into sterility.

Indeed, recent US research has revealed a dramatic slide in the ability of couples to sire/conceive children during the past two decades or more. Diet has been cited as a key cause, and this includes (but is rarely mentioned) the intake of genetically modified foods.

The small farmers of Poland, still being so numerous in spite of the best efforts of the EU and the national government to remove them, are a symbol of a new resistance. One we all need to be part of, in pushing back the forces of destruction and opening ourselves, and others, to the delights of that rich cornucopia of diversity, so often to be found under the stewardship of time-honoured guardians of a bountiful countryside.

The continued push for small farms to be 'restructured' so as to compete in the World Market—which is the mantra of the globalist neo-liberal fundamentalists—is no longer credible. It never was. The entrepreneurial skills of the artisan will ultimately endure, as the inhuman, sterile and toxic agribusiness landscape— which forms an apt canvas for the monocultural assassination of nature—falls under the sheer weight of its own lifeless, repugnant obesity.

The meeting is finally called to a close. The wording of a New Food Act, including the carefully thought through contribution supplied by our own supportive group of farmers and consumers, inches one step closer to becoming law. Inches, because new blocks to this promised land keep being placed along its route, almost without end. 'Almost' ... and it is that word which gives us heart to keep up the fight.

A fight which is, after all, for more than the survival and revival of the heroes of field and fayre. It is the fight for fundamental justice—and ultimately for life itself.

Fake food versus real food – a question of life or death

Although they might look nice, the great majority of supermarket foods are just a brilliant con trick. And I'm telling you this, sensing that the majority reading this are most likely still doing most of their food shopping in a supermarket or 'superstore'.

All right, so put on your safety belt, because I'm going to take you on a rapid ride down the aisles of that 'superstore'—the one just up the road from you.

First impression: Wow, so much choice! Wrong, the product range you are looking at is made up of many slight variations of 'one food', and that one food has a number of different manufacturers. So you go to get a litre or two of milk; Oh my! Six different mega dairies have their goods on display, all churning out the same white stuff (called milk), and they all look identical. Choice? Oh yes, you can have skimmed, reduced low fat, or whole; all of which are pasteurised and homogenised. And, of course, there's ultra-heat treated (UHT). But there's no 'milk' available. I think you get my drift: each of those products is a denatured distortion of 'real milk'. Real Milk is 'illegal' in these places—unless you're in France. Raw unpasteurised milk, with nothing added or taken out: not allowed.

Stick with me on dairy, because in many ways it's symbolic of all the rest of the junk in this 'superstore'. Did you know that 'homogenised' milk involves forcing the cream layer (which normally floats on the top) to morph into the rest of the milk? Yes, that's what happens; and it's a particularly dodgy business because this forcing is done under very high pressures, where the milk is blasted through a metal plate perforated with many small holes, thereby forcing the cream into the milk and the milk into the cream, so you can't see the difference. What comes out the other end resembles 'another food'—and by the time it's also been heat treated (pasteurised), squirted into a plastic bottle and stuck on the supermarket shelf for a few days, it is another food. Food? No sorry, shouldn't really use that term.

According to the dairy industry, the end result is supposed to be 'more attractive'. Sure, it's beautiful isn't it! Maybe, to the eyes of the advertisers. But what this 'homogenised' and pasteurised milk is doing in our gut is another thing altogether. It's essentially indigestible. So let's get serious: a report by a leading scientist/doctor in the UK some thirty years ago, exposed the fact that homogenised milk causes blockages in the arteries of the heart, leading to potential cardiac arrest. His report mysteriously disappeared soon after it was released and the author was quickly sidelined. Ever heard any stories like this before?

OK, so let's jump back on our trolley and head for the ready prepared meat department. Wow, now here's a great line up of tempting looking cuts; special ham, spicy sausages, acclaimed bacons, tender chicken nuggets and so forth. Now don't tell me there's no choice here!

Sorry, it's all coming from two or three (at the most) huge factory farms. Probably in another country or some place in your own homeland that you'd least expect. Places it would make you sick to set foot in. Places where 15,000 hens cram into one vast neon lit shed. Usually in 'cages' of eight to ten birds each. Hens fed antibiotic laced genetically modified soya and maize—and a bunch of other stuff like manioc from

Thailand and rice husks from China; whatever is cheap and available and capable of fattening a chicken in just ten weeks.

Ten weeks? Yes, that's how long it takes to get them up to slaughter weight. Just keep the lights on and keep stuffing them— and that's the full life span of a typical supermarket chicken. The antibiotics are fed prophylactically so as to keep the hens from dying of diseases which are rife in this airless, sunlight-less, neon lit 'natural' environment. Egg production: just the same horror story. Life span even shorter. Beaks clipped too. Never see grass, let alone the light of day.

Lord, give me a break! What about the pork and ham cuts on display? Yes, exactly the same regime. Hundreds, more often thousands, of pigs in the same style vast shed. Also fed GM maize and soya. Also given routine antibiotics. Also deprived of sleep and relentlessly fattened. Their life span of the fatteners is at best three to four months, and the sows maybe a year.

By way of contrast: sows on my farm, running free range on pasture, live for at least five years. Free range chickens on grass also around five to six years.

Take a look at those lovely cling film covered trays in which these remains are displayed, especially the ham. How many chemical stabilisers, synthetic preservatives and coloring agents? But listen, it can't all be that bad can it? I mean, these stores have 'quality controls' in place and very strict hygiene arrangements. Sorry, these are just sops to make you feel that the food you are buying is 'safe'. The reality is that what you are eating— unless it is certified as organic (and most 'supermarket organic' pushes the term to its limit of credibility) then you are eating the remnants of an animal that has just been through a concentration camp. Put that in your trolley? Support animal genocide?

Listen, I'm feeling a bit queasy, not sure I want to buy anything here after all—maybe just some loo roles and household detergents. Yes, of course, but the paper (unless you purchase recycled) for your loo roles is coming from strip-forest logging exercises, is heavily processed and then treated with chemicals and synthetic perfumes 'to give you a blissful toilet experience every day!' The household detergents? Do I need to tell you? Chemical paradise designed to kill anything that moves—including you!

Let's get out of here. Please don't tell me anymore. Sure, good decision—but just in case you're thinking of grabbing the odd veg for tonight's dinner. Err, well, please understand that it's almost certainly been sprayed ten to twelve times during its growing period with chemicals that destroy bees and sicken birds—so it might be better to give them a miss too, right?

Scene shifts to the supermarket car park. Orwellian looking arena, where strangely abstracted-looking people wheel their cartloads of deadly packaged produce towards shiny waiting vehicles. 'Is there any choice?' asks the by now pale-faced, shellshocked consumer.

Yes, it's called 'real food'. I suggest you grow it yourself. But I suppose you're not willing to countenance that idea. Then you must look around for the farms that do. Go to the farmers' market. Maybe to a natural foods store. Places where a human being serves you, someone who knows something about the foods on sale in their shop and where they are grown and raised.

Scale down your expectations. Look for that which is local, fresh and nourishing. Think human scale, not cyborgian mega scale. Drop the 'super' and re-find 'the market'. The market place. The real people with real smiles and earth-worn fingers. Come to your senses. Realise that you have been duped, browbeaten and robbed—maybe for years. Give your body, mind and spirit the chance to heal. Give your money to people who deserve it; people who work with, rather than against, nature. Turn over a new leaf. And if a small bug falls off it, laugh out loud—and give praise for the diversity of the living environment. Rather than the sterility of a death cult dressed-up as 'convenience'.

Julian Rose

The farmer is the future

At a farmer's fair in Krakow, South Poland, in early May, I spoke to a Romanian peasant. He was demonstrating clay pot making using a foot treadle to spin the plate upon which the pots were being formed by his deft hands.

I remarked how attractive I found this technology due to its lack of reliance upon any outside power source. He nodded, saying "No other power required." The conversation swung to the need to remain independent; independent of state and industry controlled sources of power. Because being dependent upon centralised power, be it energetic or political, means always owing something to someone or something; whereas to be free of such a burden enables one to form strategic relations where one pleases. This form of sharing creates a natural form of interdependence with fellow humans, rather than dependence on governments and corporations. He nodded again.

A colorful troupe of Gorale (Polish mountain farmers) were stamping their feet to the rousing notes of a merry fiddle while weaving a circular pattern through and amongst each other, shout-ing out in moments of bravura. My Romanian friend was looking on, his non-treadle foot tapping out the folk song's rhythms. After a little he turned towards me and said "The farmer is the future". Now this struck me as a very profound statement. Many may well cynically laugh at such an idea. In those people's minds is the notion that food will always magically appear from ... well ... somewhere – and that farmers, that is 'real farmers' like the Romanian and Polish peasants, are an anachronism, a romantic backdrop, a picture postcard of a time gone by.

The majority of people in Westernised societies have long since abandoned any attempt to source their foods from anything other than the most convenient and/or cheapest supermarket stores that carefully screen out any correlation between the end product and the grower. That, after all, might shock the buyer into realising that there still are some human hands involved in the process whereby they acquire their daily meals. It's much more comforting for them to imagine that their beloved supermarket somehow spirits their daily needs out of some super hygienic, sanitised, forever sunny, manicured Astroturf garden.

The Eastern European peasant family farmer does not know much about what goes on in the corporate run, European Union subsidised, monocultural deserts that churn out and almost endless supply of nitrate-induced, vitamin-depleted and pesticide-protected—so called 'foods'. He will not know what the majority of Westernised consumers dump into their trolleys on the way to the checkout desk, car boot and home freezer chest.

This farmer does know, however, that a very strange thing has happened to people over the past few decades. Something that seems to have taken them away from values which, to the good farmer, are pretty much sacrosanct. Values like never wasting valuable resources and living from the fruits of one's labors. About independence and love of a way of life in the open fields, open air, one that somehow keeps one always close to God.

All be it that this life pits man against hardships mostly unimaginable to the upwardly aspiring higher waged supermarket shopper. A shopper fretting that she must negotiate the precinct without her recently manicured hair suffering any distortion from the unexpected shower of rain that has afflicted the roofless car park. Ironically, that shower of rain, a few drops of which might land on her precious head of hair, is about as close to nature as this lady is ever likely to get ... in her cosseted perpetual suburban sunrise.

What the peasant farmer knows—and the consumer doesn't— is that this shower of rain is actually a vital element in the nurturing process in which he/she is engaged; growing the foods that will feed the family, and if all goes well, providing a small income from the sale of any surplus.

What this farmer also knows is that, at any time, the crops and animals under his care might be taken by drought, flood or disease. Might be threatened by wild animals, thieving individuals or interfering officialdom. This farmer lives day-in day-out with a perpetual level of uncertainty, which becomes so ingrained that it ceases to cause the sort of fear-fuelled anxieties that haunt the urbanite. Instead, it becomes an integral part of the way of life.

There is wisdom in this insecurity, because life is uncertain and unpredictable, and trusting to a degree of fate is part and parcel of our natural response to challenges that spring up without due warning.

The foundations of the supermarket society upon which our regular shopper's aspirations depend— is predicated upon a continuous and uninterrupted increase in the acquisition of wealth. It soon becomes apparent, however, that the material source of this wealth is not infinite, but finite; and that callously extracting these finite materials as though they were infinite does much damage to the fabric of the planet and brings much pollution to its vital arteries. So much so in fact, that by the beginning of the twenty-first century, alarm bells have been ringing on an almost daily basis, warning of an unprecedented crisis lurking just around the corner—unless substantial remedial action is taken.

Yet no one seems to know what form this substantial remedial action should take; because no one who participates in this consumer-driven way of life believes that 'they' could possibly be contributing to a fast-approaching global crisis! No one, that is, apart from our peasant farmer, who does not suffer an insatiable hunger for material gain, but nevertheless remains caught up in its consequences.

This farmer must pay the price for others' insistence on living in the profit-driven, fossil-fuelled fast lane of unsuppressed greed. A lane that ultimately leads to global ecocide. He will not be approached by those who depend upon the 'quality control' technicians whose role it is to scrutinise the sanitised products which line the supermarket shelves.

To these consumers, the farmer is a strangely primitive being who provokes a tremor of fear; almost disgust. Consequently, he has no buyer for his home-grown carrots and beetroots; his orchard cherries, his free-range chickens and eggs. Neither will his wife have any buyer for the fresh milk she lovingly extracts from the docile farm cow. This milk is, after all, too good to ever get into any supermarket display cabinet.

So with no one coming to the door to purchase the fruits of their labor, our farmer regretfully goes off the farm in search of some part time job to help support the family's needs. The farm activity contracts, producing just enough to feed the family. While the younger generation abandon ship in favor of earning their livelihood in another place, another country and another way of life—the one that is mining the finite wealth of the planet as though it were infinite.

Then, one day, some shocking news comes across the airwaves of the world. News that the majority of foods on sale in shops and supermarkets are unsafe to eat. That they are the cause of multiple sicknesses and unprecedented rates of cancer and heart disease. Epidemics are also spreading round the world that can no longer be controlled by conventional medicines and which the compromised human immune system is now too weak to fully resist.

A few days later it is admitted that normal resources of water have become largely undrinkable due to high levels of pesticides and hormones which have heavily polluted the rivers and streams that run through the desert-like, agrichemical-soaked monocultural farms, whose produce still lines the supermarket shelves.

In hundreds of cities and towns, panic breaks out. People desperately seek advice as to what to do and where to purchase safe foods. The big chain stores try to reassure their customers and the mainstream media calls for people to be calm and listen to the advice of government. But the story is out, and the old platitudes cease to have the desired effect.

Chaotic scenes become widespread as people become engaged in panicked attempts to stockpile what they hope are 'safe foods'. However, the truth is that no one knows what foods are safe or not safe. What water is pure or polluted. What storekeepers are honest or lying. No one had ever thought that anything like this could ever happen; so preoccupied were they with their materialistic concerns, consumer preferences and nine to five jobs. It never occurred to them that they could be collectively complicit in triggering a global crisis of unprecedented proportions.

At least, almost everybody.

Not long after this announcement was aired, a group of people nervously gathered outside our farmer's house. A woman with two young children knocked tentatively on the door; while some of the others were more openly agitated and even threatening.

The farmer came slowly to the door and opened it. "What do you want?" he said.

"I want to know if you can sell us any safe food" said the lady.

"My children are hungry and someone in the village said that on your farm the food is still not poisoned."

The farmer stood silent for a while. Others shouted out "We need food!"

Eventually he turned to his wife "Well" she said "You had better let them in."

Genetics

The war on human DNA
True humanity—or transhuman singularity and gene genocide?

We individuals are here on this planet as sentient, living beings, having the capacity to love, create, emphasise and be joyous. But these qualities are increasingly the object of a covert—if not overt—programme of systematic sterilisation and attempted eradication.

There's a war on. Not just the continuous fabricated war between nations and peoples, but a war to alter the very DNA of the human race and to thereby render homo sapiens a slave race, responding only to a computerised command system.

Don't be unduly intimidated, however, for these tricks are, like most tricks, just waiting to be exposed and rendered obsolete. Rendered obsolete by the realisation, in ourselves, of an omnipotent universal consciousness. Yes, it is we who are the ones best equipped to go face to face with our oppressors, to go forth and redeem the sanctity of life.

Witness the remarkable breakthroughs taking place within the world of quantum mechanics. Breakthroughs that reveal the fact that every cell in the human body is an intelligent being in its own right, interacting and intercommunicating for the mutual bene fit of the greater genome. The work of Bruce Lipton has brought forward a whole galaxy of compulsive information in this arena. We are here as Earthly representatives of a Divine state, an Earthly reflection of that which would otherwise remain unseen, intangible and without form: non-materialised Divine energy. Having 'form' is thus a blessed gift in which we should rejoice!

It is we who are thus gifted to take on the less than human shadow rulers of this planet—and the otherworldly parasites that prime their tanks. We, and we only. Well, not really 'only', because once we commit to the task for which we came here, unseen support floods in to help us on our way.

But we must be the first to start the ball rolling—and this takes courage. A kind of leap into the unknown. A leap that holds the promise of an unprecedented adventure to follow.

So what exactly are we up against here?

It's a pretty sophisticated box of tricks, make no mistake! At its core is the word 'subversive'. The degree to which it succeeds is the degree to which subversiveness wins over honesty. Disguise over what is real. Falsity over what is true.

This means that we cannot ourselves harbour any of these subversive tendencies, if we are to win the battle which faces us. Pretty simple isn't it?

Provided we pass that test we are in a good shape to recognise the falsity, dishonesty and subversive tendencies in others. Otherwise, clearly we aren't; and there ends our usefulness to a planet in crisis.

So the next step for those still going forward (true humanity) is becoming aware, which means seeing the big picture and both thinking and acting holistically. There's nothing special about this, it's just a question of letting that inner voice gain ground over the outer voices of indoctrination and programmed propaganda. It means conquering our cynical acceptance of a moribund status quo…You know all about this—no need to say more.

So, to return to the question: what are we really up against here?

At the most fundamental end of the subversive spectrum, we have the deliberate, clinical, laboratory alteration of the very DNA from which we are manifest as sentient beings.

At the other end of the same subversive mindset we have what is called the Transhumanist agenda: the attempt to merge human brain cell activity with 'the computer calculus', to produce an encoded, synthetic binary intelligence.

These are the twin dark prongs of absolute subversion which true humanity is confronting.

What those engaged in this Transhuman experiment are after is what they call 'the singularity'. A time when the fusion between these synthetic and 'part human' energies becomes the dominant agent over life on Earth; relegating homo sapiens to the role of slave prisoner to a man-made artifice. Not exactly a great definition of 'the good life', I think you will agree.

Meanwhile, back in the science laboratory, the gene engineers continue to pursue their ambition to push back the frontiers of moral, ethical and spiritual responsibility, by engaging in their Frankensteinian obsession with genetically engineering not just seeds, plants and animals—but humans too.

The first experiments in deletion from the human embryo of 'unwanted' human genes are awaiting the green light from governments in various Countries at this moment.

So it's important to see that the 'Transhumanists' and the 'gene engineers' are part and parcel of the same dystopian counterfeit cabal, which is simply approaching a common goal from two different angles. That goal, in case anyone needs reminding, is the construction of a pseudo-living entity that has had all its subtleties, mysteries and passions explicitly removed, so as to be tailored to conform perfectly to the demands of the designer matrix. To be a 'designer slave'.

Working backwards from these Doctor Jekyll-like sterilisers of the sentient world, we find a trail of incriminating evidence exposing their diabolical ambitions. Their sticky web can be seen spreading out into all avenues of life as it is lived today. Although 'lived' might be the wrong way to describe the dumbed-down, politically correct, conformist lifestyles adopted by great swaths of the USA, the Western World and beyond.

What we are saying here, is that our current designer societies are already constructed according to the ethos of the Transhuman, gene-altering school of subversive manipulation, and have been so for some time. Some would say for thousands of years and thanks to the intervention of a hybrid reptilian race with a need to siphon off human energies for its own ends. Ends precisely counter to the aspirations of sentient humans: true humanity.

But never mind about this, interesting speculation as it is. The point is, we are confronted here and now with this ultra manipulative, parasitic force trying to worm its way into the very foundations of life itself and to forever corrupt its essence—the living heartbeat of the Supreme Creative Principle itself.

Now if that doesn't get you on the edge of your seat shouting "Never!" probably nothing ever will.

The sycophantic thieves of divine life take their earthly form as the now infamous Illuminati, Bilderbergers, Masons and other Satanic leaning so called 'secret sects'; whose job is to ensure that their master's ambitions are steadily being met in the everyday avenues of life on planet Earth. It is their job to uphold and progress the Matrix: Big Banking, Big Pharma, Big Agro, Big Military, Big Energy, Big Transport, Big Media, Big Fashion, Big Sport, Big Entertainment, Big Atom Smasher, Big Ego—and on it goes...

Although the CEOs of these corporate behemoths may not be aware of what is driving their 'Big Ambition', they remain faithful to the implementation of the dark agenda to which they have, wittingly or unwittingly, opened themselves. It is they who ensure funding for the genetic engineering of the human food chain; the gene manipulation of the human embryo and the denaturing of the very fibre of life itself. Our governments simply rubber stamp these pre-planned secret agendas. Governments are thus also tools of enslavement.

Those who support and maintain centralised top-down power are partners in crime with those who seek to install the Singularity insanity as the ultimate salvation for this planet.

They (the top-down power mongers) take a cold and distanced perspective on others. Especially on the grounded, simple and warm-hearted. Something they have in common with the unashamed adulators of 'cyborg man'; whose idea of 'heaven on earth' is a fully automated human race, answering only to a super computer whose program software has been invented by none other than themselves; so as to anaesthetise all that is sentient, spiritual and sacrosanct about human life—indeed all of life.

So friends, that leaves us—who for the sake of this piece I am calling 'true humanity'—to carry forward the gift of Life, willingly, lovingly and courageously. We have been blessed with this task and with a very special ability that comes with it: the ability to penetrate the fortress of the pseudo-human life manipulators and take apart their master plan piece by piece; rendering it, at last, obsolete and beyond redemption.

Have no doubts—this is our reason for being. We came back to fulfil this task. We have been endowed with all that is needed to complete this mission. It is simply down to us to do it.

There is a deadline—and it is imminent. Do not fear, for we go forward joined as one in this, the greatest of all challenges. Only by fully engaging with it can we finally experience that profound awakening for which all true humanity has been striving for so long. Maybe since our inception.

Now this supreme challenge stands, unequivocally, at our very door. Open the door and welcome it with open arms.

From immaculate conception to genetic deception... leading to the rise of the crypto male

One of the things that might have given sex a bad name here on planet Earth, was the supposed arrival of highly realised beings whose conception (we are informed) did not come about via an act of conjugation between a man and a woman. Nor, one presumes, via an act of in vitro fertilisation. But by some other means. Something which, as the Bible calls 'Immaculate Conception' in the case of The Virgin Mary.

Now the word 'immaculate' suggests something without a flaw; something pure and perfect. And if the pure and the perfect are directly associated with being 'sex free' then—right from the outset—the sexual act is somehow denigrated. Denigrated as being less than pure.

So, does this mean that making progress in spiritual development has been linked, directly or indirectly, with the notion of somehow needing to rise above and beyond the act of sexual union? Beyond the expression of the duality inherent in male and female? In Yin and Yang? And in the process, has duality, as the source of sexual attraction, itself been reduced to that which needs to be 'overcome' rather than celebrated?

These are big questions indeed, but vital ones to get a handle on. Not to turn away from lest they should reveal the existence of some long-lost truths capable of turning our accepted views upside down.

Let's explore this avenue of thought with open hearts and minds and see where it leads.

For something of flesh and blood to come to life without a male sperm or a female egg coming into the picture at all, would probably fit the description of 'a miracle'. The word 'miracle' and the word 'miraculous' have the same origin. They refer to that which is "not explained by known laws of nature" (dictionary definition).

Beyond that which is conceived as possible.

In the story of Jesus' birth, the Bible informs us that Jesus was 'born of the Virgin Mary'. And it is due to this event having taken place that the birth has been tagged as 'miraculous': an immaculate conception. After all, how could sperms and eggs be involved if Mary was deemed to have remained a virgin at the time of the birth of her son?

In some African tribal societies, it is believed that lightning confers upon woman the wherewithal to bring a child into the world. Nature can be wildly fecund under the electric conductivity present during intense thunderstorms. Could some potent yet unrecognised seed be awakened in a receptive female during such an event? Could it ripen into the embryonic form of a human baby?

In currently fashionable 'electric universe' theories, who knows what super-charged electrons and neutrons might not get up to!

One thing I've learned in my steadily increasing time here on planet Earth, is never to dismiss out of hand that which at first seems inexplicable. There is so much we don't understand about almost everything, let alone the small matter of how life comes (or came) to be. In fact, as regards the origin of our universe, purely 'rational science' has got us almost nowhere, swinging to and fro between big bangs and a bunch of barking quarks!

Yet there might be an all together more simple and plausible explanation for the immaculate nature of the so called 'virgin birth'. One whose exploration leads us into the vexed yet critically important world of semantics. Semantics as being the key without which we cannot unlock the hidden agendas that have long since been screened out of our perceptions—due to their wholly revolutionary nature. Due to their power to turn the world we think we comprehend on its proverbial head.

Imagine that a new angle on the meaning of one word could be the detonator for an entirely fresh understanding of who we are and why we're here. That the deliberate linguistic obfuscation of original intentions and writings just might turn out to be the biggest bang in the Bible!

What if the Virgin Mary was not actually a virgin at all—in our normal understanding of this word—but an ascendant woman of great spiritual power and purity?

Her son, Jesus, being conceived in the way nature intended via Mary's union with Joseph; a suggestion which, in fact, is no longer the least bit controversial.

However, Mary 'the virgin' takes on a dramatically more illustrious and enlightened meaning once we have banished the old unbroken hymen—seal of purity—dogma.

And here I am most indebted to a colleague, Claire, Art Editor of International Times, for bringing to my awareness this truly liberating interpretation of the original meaning of the word 'virgin' within the context of the mythological status accorded to the Virgin Mary, mother of Jesus. A myth which has dogged the female of our species pretty much since the dawn of history; and thereby caused both men and women to suffer massive misconceptions about what, why—and even who—we are.

So here is what Claire wrote, as a comment to my essay on the 'Original Sin':

"Mary was a woman of high spiritual standing, an ascended being. This was not an uncommon thing in the time of Jesus (who had similar women in his own ministry) but there was no word for such a woman in the Western language when the Bible was being translated from Paleo-Hebrew or Aramaic. The closest word for a spiritually pure, wise and enlightened woman was "virgin", which of course means something entirely different in Western terms, and has been a huge historical deception which has reinforced the patriarchal agenda down through the ages.

Similarly, Mary Magdalene was construed as a prostitute when at the time women had no choice, as slaves, but to be so under Roman rule. The only other option was freedom which often meant social exclusion and abject poverty, where death was preferable. Two more myths of history which need addressing."

Others picked up on this disclosure adding to the dialogue sparked by Claire's intervention. Comments by women willing to speak out honestly and deeply about the third-rate status accorded to their gender since time immemorial, due to a deliberate long-standing debasement of woman's true role within (and without) the male/female partnership. To this I must add the distortion of the meaning and role of the female essence which resides in the male, and for that matter, the male essence which lies in the female.

This is such a profound subject—I hardly know how to do it justice. But we men must make that effort. We have an absolutely vital role to play now in supporting the emancipation of the women of our planet. And this starts with the recognition and emancipation of the female within ourselves.

We men cannot progress on our journey of personal growth until we honour that which provides us with our spiritual raison d'être. I state that outright because it is the truth. Within the realm of 'partnership' women cannot become 'realised' women until men become 'realised' men through honouring the woman in themselves.

I explored in some depth in 'Original Sin—A Myth Whose Time Is Up' the nature of duality as the essential catalytic force of the universe. Duality being: female and male essence as the friction-inspired driving force of movement and change; that which stands behind evolution itself.

I argue that this is not something 'to overcome' or 'get beyond', as some spiritual aspirants believe; but to be fully embraced for what it is, and accepted as inseparable from our divine origins. That until this is fully achieved, and the old superimposed sexual guilt trip abandoned and laid to rest, we cannot find our—centred— place within. And will always be circling restlessly around the truth instead of becoming it. Letting it be.

If 'the virgin' is indeed correctly identified as signifying a deeply enlightened and therefore sexually aware woman, then we had better admit that some seriously devious force has played a very dark, and yet quite brilliant trick on mankind, the repercussions of which are almost beyond imagination. A trick performed by twisting the word 'virgin' into something wholly other than what was intended.

Once again it is religion and the church which reveal themselves to be the chief accomplices in spreading the falsified version that has so thoroughly colonised our planet over the millennia. The same duo that foisted 'Original Sin' and 'the dark side baptism' on our browbeaten humanity.

So, to recap: by placing the Virgin Mary on a pedestal of 'sexual purity' the perpetrators were able to ensure that all other womanhood would be tainted, having resorted to the (impure) act of sexual union in order to bear children. As only a truly divine being, it is implied, can be born by a route which avoids any involvement in the sexual act.

So it follows that: those who aspire towards spiritual purity and union with Godhead must be taught to avoid, wherever possible, sex and sexual communion. For in this skewed interpretation it is clearly a severe deviant to the route to purity and Godliness. A route to all that is deemed undignified, debased and denigrating within humanity's aspirations.

This a truly massive act of sabotage of all that manifests itself as a glorious expression of universal life. A dastardly attempt to neuter and render sinful that which is in fact the very wellspring of life itself. The very dynamo of our expansive and ever expanding cosmos. This is all-out war on the life force. An attempt to render sterile the very seed from which all life has sprung. From this deception has followed the vast unfolding of a pervasive death cult. A cult whose roots lie in the blatant denigration of the female. A denigration and sterilisation of primal female power, which opened the way for the consequent rise into almost unassailable power of 'the crypto male'; a (genetically) crippled species whose aims, ideologies and actions are an expression of a dehumanised entity primed to go to war. A war which starts within, due to the ostracising and demonising of the female in itself.

But because this denial is itself denied, the war quickly turns outward and becomes a war against humanity and against nature herself. Nature, whose diversity and beauty can only be experienced and celebrated by an animated and healthily balanced female/male principle, freely and joyously at play within each one of us.

Look how this half-man has laid waste to our planet. Unleashing a monotone depravity upon the spontaneous biodiversity of nature. Ripping through eons of health embracing plant life and raping our soils of their lifegiving fertility. Then, as if this wasn't enough, dispensing a toxic soup of carcinogenic killer sprays over what remains of the life-giving properties that form the foundation of the human, animal and insect food chain.

But even then crypto male cannot call a truce; but must go on to genetically modify the DNA of the planetary gene pool itself, so as to stamp his transhumanist predispositions onto the blueprint of elementary life.

All the while, in our societies of denial, these nefarious acts of murder have been declared to be 'progress'. Examples of ever more 'efficient' ways of controlling planetary life, including that of other human beings. Of devising ever more 'smart' ways of making sure than nothing, but nothing, escapes the now ubiquitous 'silent weapons for quiet wars'. Weapons that symbolise the male in denial of the female within—and without. Crypto man: the ultimate Mr. Male; able to perform even an unfeeling act of genocide on his own duality! Hail to our Rambo! Surely the mark of a REAL man... Enough, enough, lest I drown in the bottomless pool of my own indignation.

But how has the feminine survived at all? How has that which has been under the sword for so long managed to maintain a wick and even a flame, in spite of all? The answer is that the baton of Real Life has somehow been passed on and on even in the midst of torture and tyranny. The power of the female is irrepressible. She cannot be put down.

Even with every emasculated gun-slung terminator on the planet running on a full tank of dark-fuelled adrenalin, female essence cannot be destroyed. But like the medicinal clovers of blessed old cow pastures, grows new leaves and new flowers however many times she is reduced to just a seed buried in the tarnished ground.

However, let us not romanticise the true reality of life under the twisted tyrannical regimes that continue to rule our planet. So desperate are they to possess, dominate and control the elusive feminine spirit—the spirit of love— that we have to be super alert to every top down move emanating from their despotic power pyramid. Obsessed as they are with masterminding mechanisms for monitoring every last element of societies' activities, lest some spark of truth should ignite a rebellion.

A rebellion that would turn the tide on the dominance of controlling mechanisms that ripple on via the deluge of hi-tech interference now proliferating our planet. Even to the extent of distorting the natural Schuman Resonance upon which we all depend in order to establish an inner harmony with universal forces.

But in spite of all these tools of oppression, there is an air of desperation about this frenetic behaviour. All is not so well in the crypto male camp. In fact, there is a sense of insecurity creeping into its once super dominant 'New World Order' blueprint. For the sparks of truth are taking hold, and we men are losing faith in the old model of what it means to 'be a man'. We are listening to other voices now. Voices that come from another place. A place we had been taught to associate with 'weakness', but which in fact turns out to be the place where resides our greatest strength. Our intuitive and receptive nature. Our true guide to a still largely unexplored universe of potentiality.

That is the place where every day and at all times, we walk amongst the joyous manifestations of truth, and in the blink of an eye, are able to determine that which is fake and that which still manifests itself as part of the old lie.

For so long the male thought that 'conquering' nations; 'conquering' nature and then 'conquering' space, were the indisputable prerogatives of the male ego. But all of this was the grand illusion of grand illusions. Aeons of death and destruction, and all because of an ingrained fear of the divine female principle. Our guide to deeper truth. The female side of the male. A fear put in place by forces in whose interests it was (is) to separate and to divide against itself, the essentially inseparable male/female duality which is our Universe.

Due to the extraordinary power that the concept of 'Immaculate Conception' held over human society, the emancipation of woman was lost before it could even be begun. And what hope for a realised man without a realised woman to partner him? What chance of a holistic expansion of homo sapiens when holism itself is neutered at birth?

And woman, for so long accused of being the one to bring man down—or of being a witch because she occasionally expressed her true powers—eventually resorted to imitating the male in an attempt to break free of her chains.

But the only chains that got at least partially broken were the ones that surrounded the male enclave; thus allowing woman to enter his world, but not allowing man to enter hers. Sadly, much of the feminist movement expressed that entanglement under the slogan 'women's liberation'. But the true woman, as with the true man, has no part in that worn old male world, and is still emerging; taking a form which we have glimpsed in bursts of enigmatic and energetic status quo table turning.

In the end, and inevitably, men and women are all entangled in the web of divide, conquer, separate and destroy. The only way out of this is to gain some deeper understanding of this predicament. To recognise it honestly as the central dilemma that it is, and see how this falsehood has infiltrated and taken control of every avenue of daily life on planet Earth.

In writing this, I have tried to explore and expose the powers of the words and symbols that lie behind the heinous disruption of human evolution. It is the twin towers of Church and Religion that emerge as the chief controlling influence over doctrines devised specifically to send us on at least a two millennia detour from our original and true trajectory.

Much of humanity has suffered from the results: a deliberate poisoning and denaturing of that which is our true guiding force for attaining heightened knowledge and deeper awareness. We have been deviated from experiencing the acts of inception, procreation and birth as the natural microcosmic mirror of the macrocosmic universal birth cycle. A celebration of God's profound inventiveness.

No one ever needed, or wanted, a 'virgin birth' or an 'immaculate conception' to be the unattainable standard bearer for human aspiration. No one ever needed to believe that the loving act of union between man and woman, or between Shiva and Shakti, was in some way sinful.

No one, that is, except that which at some point acquired the need to vampire divine energy so as to sustain its artful and artificial subterfuge. A subterfuge which has gone largely unrecognised (as a subterfuge) by the great swath of humanity to this day. Yes, a semantic subterfuge. One achieved by subverting and reversing the meaning of words. Words like 'virgin' and 'immaculate'. And attempting in the process, to trick the human mind into nullifying, sterilising and rendering obsolete all that which springs from the divine love affair of which we are the human manifestation.

Now we return to this unashamed source of love! Bearing overflowing offerings of gratitude for having been gifted with our blessed male and female essence; and the insight, intuition and passion to take this extraordinary planet through the gathering apocalypse, and on to the rebirth of a world swept clean of its bloated vampiric energy thieves.

Onward, onward, onward we go, tasked with nurturing into existence a reawakened world. A world in which the dynamic of balance will stand out from the sterile disunity of yesterday.

Man or Robot?

More on the transhumanist singularity

Bear with me, for this may not be an easy read—but we need to work further on the cracking of the code of this much discussed chimera.

Which is not to say it doesn't exist—it does. Yet it exists as a by-product of minds that operate in a subhuman vacuum; that have severed their connection with the normal diversity of emotions, and more particularly with spirit and soul. Once this type of divorce is sanctioned there can only be deleterious consequences. The current Transhumanist ethos is deeply atheistic, and as such has no need to replace God, since it doesn't believe there is such an entity in the first place. But, ironically, it seemingly does have the need to create an all-powerful god of its own particular design.

Such a concept, pursued through to its conclusion, can, according to its proponents, provide some sort of final solution to the human dilemma. So we get the Transhumanist notion that the realisation of a computer that can outmanoeuvre the human brain will somehow produce a liberated society.

Nothing, in reality, could be further from the truth. By handing over responsibility for the management of our lives to machines, we usurp our own ability to shape, alter, direct and ultimately rejoice in the art of living.

Instead, we individually elect to become slaves to our own inventions.

Recognising this is most important, as it puts the Transhumanist agenda in its true light—which is actually not light at all—but essentially dark. When given free rein, harboring delusion al visions of power leads on to openly fascistic expressions. The Nazi eugenics program of World War Two is testimony to this horror. And the attempt to bring into existence an all-powerful 'conscious' computer capable of outstripping human intelligence makes Transhumanism into a new form of concentration camp.

The eugenics school of 'population cleansing' has never been far from the surface in this corporate dominated era, and is particular to those who harbor New World Order ambitions. But to achieve a major depopulation ambition in the post World War II era would require a highly subversive sleight of hand, and I believe that the Transhumanist prophecy of a coming 'Singularity' is such a deeply subversive sleight of hand.

Transhumanists use the term 'the Singularity' to describe the time when they believe that artificial intelligence, in continuing on its exponential rate of growth, will take over—or overtake—natural intelligence. They name that time 'The Omega Point'.

This is, I suggest, a direct plagiarism of the spiritual context in which this same term (although not in common parlance) would describe the time of humanity's broad awakening to Divine Consciousness or Godliness.

The Singularity of Transhumanist origins thus represents the demonic opposite of Divine Awakening, or Enlightenment. It reverses the natural flow of life and imprisons its prey in a Matrix-like world of brainwashed, sterile conformity; the overseer of which is a man-made brain. Orwell, Huxley and others warned of just such a possibility more than sixty years ago.

So when we hear that Google, whose chairman is a regular Bilderberg secret society attendee, is pursuing interests in this field, it becomes all too clear that the agenda is directly linked to the ongoing establishment of just such a big brother global control system. One which, according to the Singularity ethos, ultimately leads on to a technically refined form of 'thinking' super-computer permanently replacing the higher callings of the human mind. Under this heinous regime, it is touted that this piece of man-made technology will, sooner or later, take the responsibility for managing planetary affairs completely out of human hands, and leave newly 'liberated' people to scuttle around like so many rudderless chickens under the watchful eye of the 'master cyborg cock'.

The software instructions would no doubt gear this all-pervasive big brother to instil a further degree of fear upon an already jittery society. And so in awe of its powers would people be, that the 'logic' of its pronouncements/actions would be deemed irrefutable. So much so, that all its instructions could never be proved invalid, or be capable of being struck down by a court of law.

No surprise that we have recently witnessed a slew of cinematic previews of this futuristic type of scenario becoming reality. If you have ever tried to question your account balance with banking staff, you will likely have experienced an abdication of responsibility for any error that may have been made, followed by a reference to any error being "with the computer" and therefore somehow beyond the control of bank staff. This is an initial phase of human abdication to the 'thinking' machine. Only a managerial employee might finally be persuaded to actually check the com-puting end of the system for a potential error.

The desire to never be held accountable and to escape all personal responsibility for the realisation of one's own God-given creative potential or for the condition of the physical world, represents the ultimate escapist agenda; and it makes perfect cannon fodder for the vampiric greed of a totalitarian control system.

We know that various forms of high-tech (mind) control systems were already under scrutiny in the USA, within the sinister and secretive MK-Ultra programme and CIA sponsored Cybernetics teams of four or five decades ago. And that before this, certain pseudo-Christian sects held that the gathering of all human intelligence into one vast central holding pool would somehow provide the basis for an evolutionary shift into a higher evolved state for humankind, which would in turn flood the universe with the power of its combined intelligence.

Within this delusional homophobic vision of a man-made speeded-up evolution, the 'superior mind' of the computer would be relied upon to corral collective global human information energy. Once achieved, it would no doubt be left in charge of deciding who would—and who would not—be acceptable to the resulting cybernetic society. A super-computer would, in this way, inherit the role of eugenics commander-in-chief, and in something like a Scientology debriefing session, would be given responsibility for selecting who was eligible or ineligible within a kind of sub-human 'survival of the fittest'. The ineligible being dispensed with in whatever way was deemed 'most efficient'.

Most efficient and most in keeping with the needs of those taking part in the designing and programming of the commander-in-chief's software, who would be sure to write themselves out of the program and claim that they had no part in the outcome. This super-computer will therefore supply the perfect alibi as, according to its programmers, it will have exceeded their ability to retain control over its actions—and thereby absolve them from responsibility for its excesses. The ultimate preconceived opt-out. Nevertheless, the commander-in-chief computer's primary role is supposed to be a triggering of the great 'Singularity Event'. An event that might manifest itself as some kind of Luciferian/Illuminati glorification rapture. A ritualistic dark-side fest with strong similarities to the annual Bohemian Grove gathering in California. A satanic coming together to celebrate the time in which the spiritual soul would finally be laid to rest and the rampant materialist ambitions of a soulless elite get their full and unopposed due. In this scenario 'The Omega Point' sees the New World Order and Illuminati dream fulfilled.

After this, the machine would no doubt be switched off, by someone who had retained sufficient will power to carry out this action. Most of the new inheritors of the Earth would insist on having human slaves to look after their various and vicarious needs. In their compassionless version of Shangri La, the suffering of others would likely add some 'frisson' to daily life, and robotic objects could not so amply fulfil this role.

It seems likely that today's Transhumanists are extending a script that emanates from the Nazi era. The wish to preserve/ build a super race and rid the world of all that fails to measure up to its definitions of mental perfection. Illuminati initiates already consider themselves to be bloodline descendants of extra-terrestrial god-kings. These extra-terrestrial ambitions tie in closely with the Transhuman agenda, in which human heart based spiritual power, being the chief obstruction to the fulfilment of their goal, is finally fully subverted.

We know something about this. For the same sinister theme runs throughout the barely hidden ambitions of corporate exploits in the fields of GMO, pharmaceuticals, agrichemicals, nuclear energy, much of the food industry, corporate-controlled media, key banking institutions, advanced technology and telecommunications, the military-industrial project, NATO, the super-rich and the top dogs of just about all government institutions including the Vatican and other church hierarchies. Not forgetting the European Union and United States executive and taking in the World Bank, the World Trade Organisation and all the main global trading blocs of this materialistically segmented planet.

In all these—and more—one can detect the mostly secretive, but sometimes quite open despotic desire to exercise an inhuman form of domination, surpassing even the profit motive. The desire to exercise a coldly controlling influence over others and to use this planet as if it were nothing more than free fuel for the further aggrandisement of already over-inflated egos. Never mind if ecocide is the end result. Never mind if wisdom, knowledge and a caring heart have to be dispensed with in order to get this devil onto its vainglorious throne.

All these sinister ambitions are fully dependent for their realisation on the Singularity 'Omega Point' delivering its technological takeover of human society and mesmerising the majority into submission and surrender with its seemingly endless and adaptable calculating capacities.

Psychologically, the despotic 'thinking super-computer' is nothing more than the projection of an ever-restless alter ego. A compensation for an unbearable sense of spiritual inner emptiness and the attempt to try to make up for this by surrendering one's soul to an all-powerful and dominating self-created idol.

So if you harbour a secret fascination of corporate mass produced gadgetry—watch out! You are already entering the foothills of the Transhumanist domain and opening yourself to a mind controlling medium which is shaping the lives of a whole generation even as I write.

It is, in fact, part of the same domain in which avid genetic scientists like Craig Venter are putting the final touches to their (ostensibly illegal) laboratory conceived designer babies.

We, in whom circulates the precious red blood of love, sympathy, sadness, joy and passion, are never going to fall foul of this soulless ghost—neither now nor in the future. But we need to know about it—if only to remind ourselves of what lies in store for this world if we fail to realise our God-given potential to live fully as warm-hearted, creative beings.

Creative, sentient beings whose destiny is to break through the insanity which surrounds us, drawing upon a deeper courage and a greater conviction concerning our own Divine powers. Powers to bring forth that which will banish forever those who count on fear winning out over the glorious celebration of love, which is, has been, and will always be, the true foundation of Universal and Earthly life.

The anatomy of cyborg man 'Overcoming the Robotic Mind'

In 'The Transhumanist Singularity', I attempted to address the supposedly imminent takeover of humanity by a computer-controlled technology designed by people who have let their free will be usurped by that of a machine.

It became evident during the research into the background to the Transhumanist agenda, that not only 'eugenics' but also 'reductivism— the reducing of all human life to a gene—is a central component of the techno anti-life blueprint.

I am thankful for William Engdahl in pointing out that after World War II and the horrors of Auschwitz, the term 'eugenics' acquired a bad reputation, and the name was changed to 'genetics': which, as in reductivism, is about the reducing of human life to a gene. This enables genetic engineers to manipulate the expression of that gene so that it becomes dominant and takes complete control over other life forms.

Here we find a direct connection with GMO: the altering of a plant's or animal's genetic make-up in order to program into it a set of reactions designed to fit the requirements of corporatised global agriculture. Requirements in which nature's way of doing things is deemed inferior to man's; and genetic reprogramming, via laboratory intervention, superior to discovering and working together with the unfolding pulse of universal creation.

In this we see the cyborg mentality clearly emerging, with its seemingly fixated tunnel vision mentality wedded to an advanced state of delusional hubris. In truth, this is an apt enough definition of clinical insanity.

However, the reason why the social services do not rush to the rescue of those suffering from this sort of dementia, is that the system in which such services operate is itself deeply influenced by the same underlying sickness. Varying degrees of clinical insanity are prevalent throughout all areas of the status quo, leading to the fact that 'mad scientist syndrome' does not stand out sufficiently strongly from what surrounds it to attract undue or special attention.

Given that this is the case, we must conclude that a great part of society is already captive to a creeping robotic sickness which is part and parcel of the general dumbing-down program to which humanity has succumbed over recent decades.

I wish to make reference here to a comment made by a perceptive reader. The paragraph quoted is part of a longer comment, but is sufficiently succinct to stand alone as an expression of the intent of the author:

"Transhumanism is nothing more than using technology to progressively exceed all the limitations, flaws, mistakes and genetics that amount to poor design which we were born as prisoners into and had no say about.

I think the people that want the world of inherited sickness, injury-potential, degeneration of ageing (and death itself) and scarcity are the crazy ones. Since there seems to be no god loving enough to correct all these flaws no matter how many billions of prayers are ever uttered it sort of goes without saying that practical Transhumanists have no alternative except to resort to technology and their own work and research to try and fix these failings." It would be easy to dismiss this statement as just the cynical outpouring of a techno-obsessed nerd. However, upon closer inspection, it reveals a way of thinking which is common to many science and finance trained minds operating behind the scenes today. Particularly one should note the author's view that we are all born into a world of 'poor design' full of 'limitations, flaws, mistakes and genetic traits' to which we are 'prisoners' and have no say about.

Transhumanists, the author states "have no alternative except to resort to technology and their own work and research to try and fix these failings."

While this is obviously a case of 'man playing God'—one has to remind one's self that the Transhumanist does not believe in any form of supreme entity. It is technical proficiency, leading to a perfection of emotionless functionality, which is instead held to be the supreme goal of the human race. That state would presumably fit the bill of having ironed out all the flaws inherent in the original design.

This dream of mechanised flawless robotic perfection links with Newtonian physics. In Newton's theory, the spheres move mechanically across the heavens providing an absolute order in which everything falls into place with predictable clockwork precision. If such an arrangement were to be seen as somehow of superior efficiency to a world guided by the variability of human emotions, physiques and degrees of impurity, then one can see why certain schools of science might declare man to be a 'poor design' and generally inferior to the surety and safety provided by the Newtonian model.

Computers also offer the safety and predictability of a Newtonian design which 'obeys' a mechanistic principle. To those who suffer a deep fear of the unknown and who have never sampled—or have rejected— the warm and loving characteristics inherent in humanity, a computerised overlord offers a kind of safe haven. Complete predictability, born out of a multiplication of sexless logical algorithms, is the same psychology that much of modern advertising uses to sell its 'perfect couples' with their 'perfect toothpaste tube smiles' and 'perfect children', 'perfect house' and of course 'perfect weed-free garden.' Not to mention all other perfect packaged consumables which supermarkets have redesigned as an expression of the mind control methodology Edward Bernays first brought into prominence in the USA during the 1920's.

The concept of 'perfection'—defined as something in which all 'traits' have been removed, is thus the model of cyborgian man. For that vision to gain widespread traction, its creators have to first define what 'the problems' are (that need removing) and then come up with a rarefied model of a 'problem-free' look-alike. Then, using the devious powers of modern advertising— attract the masses to imitate (or purchase) this model.

Such a trait to a supermarket is for example, a curved banana. Because one cannot fit as many curved bananas onto a standard supermarket shelf as largely straight bananas. Here we see how the logic of profit driven mass production demands the alteration of nature in order to comply with its objectives.

Once such a formula is set in motion, the public must then be made to believe that such foods are 'superior' to those that don't conform to this particular vision of perfection. This is achieved by indoctrination: conveying the impression that trait-free 'healthy' bananas grow straight and that all others are inferior. The straighter the banana the more pure it is and the more easily identifiable with some form of purified genetic stock. A direct continuation of the Nazi eugenics formula for the ascension of the blond-haired, blue-eyed 'Übermensch'.

If you cast your mind over the format for the materialistic modern world, you will recognise the replication of this mass-production standardised formula everywhere you look; and in the case of the globalised food industry the takeover is almost complete.

In fact monoculture, the agrichemically assisted continuous growing of one or two types of crop on the same land year after year to the exclusion of any other species, is straight out of the 'man playing God' manual.

Using toxic chemicals to achieve the complete exclusion of nature's expression in favor of man's, has been responsible for an unprecedented decline of natural biodiversity on a global scale for the past century or more. So when genetically modified seeds and plants are introduced into already agrichemically dominated monocultures, to the instigator it is no more than the continuation of an existing pattern of 'man over nature' innovations. But follow it through and one sees that the ultimate end game is a complete takeover of the food chain. One in which a man-made and -controlled intervention ensures that nature's predications and inclinations are one hundred percent excluded.

Do you see how this exactly parallels the Transhumanist ambitions for Cyborg man?

What I am suggesting is that Cyborg man is already present in the majority of top-down hierarchical scientific and quasi scientific ambitions. And within the institutions that make up the kernel of the Military Industrial Complex, global banking, energy and pharmaceutical monoliths, not to mention governments acting as the 'democratic stewards' of the whole infernal circus.

We can only effectively counteract this cyborgian mindset by understanding how it ticks; getting under its skin and then subverting it. Ultimately, we find that the 'masters of control' influence—pervasive throughout the political status quo—reveals a line of connection to certain Masonic/Luciferian ambitions and practices into which the cyborg mentality neatly fits. This in turn leads back to the extra-terrestrial god-kings whom Illuminati initiates claim an extended blood-line connection with.

Could it be that these Transhumanist and cyborg devotees are responding to an (as yet uninterrupted) line of instruction that emanates from interbreeding Illuminati power worshippers?

If so, it could explain a lot about why they would believe that sentient human existence is full of 'limitations, flaws and genetic mistakes' and why the only way to overcome these 'failures' is to bring life under the control of a technologically refined robot programmed to simulate the human, but with all elements that deviate from a Godless algorithmically programmed cyborg, systematically removed.

Here lies a great clue for us who carry the torch of real humanity onward. It is our imperative to free ourselves and those whom we seek to make aware, from any influence that this alien underworld may hold. For it is a world whose sinister deviations from the Tao of deeper human destiny are the work of dark side quasi-geniuses. Those whose reversed logic carries within it a very real appeal to the weak-minded and spiritually impoverished and whose extraordinary self-sustained arrogance makes it appear impregnable to the true forces of universal love, art and all forms of joyous aspiration.

Under these circumstances we are called upon to fully open up untapped powers in ourselves and in others. Powers which are the key to overcoming all attempts to hijack the human race and this planet Earth, our home. That is the imperative of this time.

We are faced by a challenge which is the ultimate challenge of all challenges: to overcome the temptation to be seduced into failing to rise to the Godly qualities with which we have been endowed from birth. The only qualities that ensure certain victory for that which is allied to the Divine.

For we will undoubtedly need to draw upon that extraordinary well-spring if we are to overcome the cyborg mentality which is its chief opposite.

In this deeply perplexing, unfathomable and yet wondrous game called life, these two forces now stand head to head. We have arrived at the final door. A door which determinedly blocks the full emancipation of the human condition. Rise to the challenge of pushing open this door and we will become an unstoppable force, no matter what further obstructions are thrown in our path.

The re-engineering of life

What do atmospheric aerosol geo-engineering, the genetic engineering of foods and the reordering of the human genome have in common?

They are all part of an attempt to alter the fundamental building blocks of life and to put in their place an artificial substitute that is one hundred percent subject to the will of its owner-controllers.

Clearly these owner-controllers fully believe their personal vision of 'the perfect life' to be greatly superior to any other. But no megalomaniac knows that he is a megalomaniac, so unless physically removed from their position of influence, much damage can be expected to result.

Many of us today puzzle over the weird, surreal even, diversion that life appears to have taken to have allowed such anti-life authoritarian figureheads to gain any traction at all on this planet. Not just to espouse their insane visions, but to actually garner enough support to set them in motion.

Does their gaining such a substantial command over the workings of society expose a fundamental weakness at the core of humankind? A subconscious predilection to close the eyes and brain to that which lies beyond immediate domestic and self-interested concern?

While such a kink in humankind might tell some of the story, it does not tell the whole story; although there are obvious grounds for arriving at such a simplistic conclusion. Not least the fact that various forms of intellectual laziness are—and have been—fashionable for a long time. And if people don't want to be seen as 'different' they will go to great lengths to fit into the accepted pattern of the day, decade, century.

They will be content to be slaves rather than carry forward the torch of truth. And this is fecund ground for the rise and rise of the power-monger, who may find little resistance to his manipulative skills and attendant desire to dominate. Even distorted nature abhors a vacuum, so the fact that some exploitative element would occupy the vacant seat could almost be considered inevitable.

However, it is not inevitable that whatever or whoever occupies the vacant seat must be a life-exploiter rather than a life-supporter. Neither is it inevitable that the majority of humankind should spend the greater part of their lives in a state of abject slumber.

It is far more likely that much of what recent researchers 'down the rabbit hole' have brought back to the surface is broadly true: namely, that most varieties of megalomania are the result of a conditioned, disciplined school of control-freak persuasion. With direct connections to hierarchical 'god-king' lines of ancestry linking royal bloodlines, powerful fiefdoms and strongholds of religious fanaticism, going back centuries.

A critical factor in the maintenance of the dark empires that symbolise the obsessive unipolar power of these lines, is the desire to keep all powers and possessions tightly tethered within a small number of connected family units.

I have a degree of insider information concerning this, as I was brought up within the British upper-class world that takes such powers for granted. The landed estates of the wealthy, well connected elites, are quite simply fortresses that act to reinforce their owners' belief in themselves as 'best leaders'. Little empires, having all the qualities that depopulationists and corporate kings crave.

The largest royal bloodline fiefdoms are quite literally isolated from the outside world. Thus they 'become the world' for those that inherit and maintain them. Such people will be found at the core of most of the political think tanks of Europe and North America. They go to the same universities, share the same clubs and mix within the same social milieux.

Thus one gets the 'two world' phenomenon that divides by money and class, the societies of the Western world and beyond. It is here that what is divisive and sinister gets to work.

Not only is inter-family marriage put in place to safeguard the accumulated wealth, but so is the engineering of human, animal and plant DNA also indulged in for the same ends. To invent and to patent a 'novel' life form is to acquire control and ownership of it in perpetuity.

In the inner sanctum, plans are hatched that will ensure ownership of the world by 'a chosen few'. The powers that they accord to themselves are almost limitless, that is why bankers sit at the pinnacle of the elite cabal pyramid. They arrange the world's finances so that the collateral and the cash lands up in their pockets. This is the debt slavery system to which we all subscribe. At least nearly all. It ensures the longevity of the elite blood lines and their highly acquisitive ambitions.

It is the fuel that keeps the world in a perpetual state of division and war. And it is overseen and protected by a legal system whose key officers are closely vetted members of the same club.

It's a club that finances both the 'terrorists' and the 'anti-terrorists' at the same time.

A club that divides, conquers and kills until all the fear-struck survivors can do is shout "For God's sake leave us alone—give us peace!" And all this we are paying for. I repeat—all this we are paying for. We are conspicuous in our complicity to support that which we abhor. Most of us.

So the way to do something truly meaningful, which goes beyond the accusing and hand-wringing, is to take our money out of the all-powerful banking and stock market trading corporations. As it is these institutions that form the bedrock of the elitist control system which holds a synthetically engineered sword over our lives, as well as the subtle living exigence of planet Gaia herself.

Invest it in something worthy, ethical and of real value to the future. I made this move some years ago. It removes a major hypocrisy from our efforts to walk the road of truth.

If you have any financial resources, other than what is needed for day to day necessities, use them to support that which is humane and opposes the neo-liberal globalised free trade scam that finances the re-engineering of life on this planet, and steamrolls into oblivion everything of value that stands in its path.

This is the most straightforward and pragmatic action we can perform if we are serious about taking apart the phoney fiat financial scam that fuels the global cabal's megalomania.

It is, in large part, our feeble-minded fear of a loss of personal convenience and security that holds us back from taking the steps that must be taken to ameliorate conditions on this planet.

If we don't take our money out of 'the system' it will be stolen from us anyway, by the system—for the system. Yes, its protagonists will quite simply raid your bank account and help themselves. The 'bail-in'. It already happened on Cyprus and it will happen in all places where bankers hold the reins of power. And frankly, that is pretty much everywhere that is hooked into the global economy.

To prevent the re-engineering and retarding of life we must collapse that which supports its insanity. We will suffer forever under the stigma of a deep hypocrisy if we fail to take steps that can save this planet and all that moves on it from a fate one hundred times worse than death.

This truth is uncompromising and unavoidable. We must act on it—and act now.

Technology that Deceives

Smart phones and stupid people

Surely no one can have failed to notice: engineered electronic intelligence in pocket-sized parameters is a formidable little weapon of potential mass destruction.

However, one must not make assumptions, since most of humanity has so far failed to notice that atmospheric aerosol geo-engineering is a weapon of mass destruction, I guess it should come as no surprise that 'smart' cell phones remain largely unrecognised as the little mind-bombs that they are.

Not the sort of bombs that cause vast explosions—that form of destruction may be close to past its sell-by date for those who would engineer our futures. No need, after all, to blow us all to hell if we are perfectly happy to go there quietly, of our own accord. And many millions seem ready to do just that; led by the Pied Piper of convenience technology.

For there is a strange world out there, a virtual world to which literally billions of people are now addicted, finding it indispensable to their daily routines.

The madness of geo-engineering our climate and smartphone engineering our brains, is linked. Put superficially, the more you look down at your flickering gizmo the less likely you are to look up to witness the engineered cloud formations grid-lining our once blue skies. Or for that matter, the beauty and subtlety of nature or the grace and dignity of fine architecture.

In fact, a disposition towards 'not seeing' has been on the rise for at least two or three decades now. It applies to vaccinations, GMO's, food additives, radiation, electro smog and so many more creeping weapons of the 'silent wars' assailing our planet and our physiological and mental capacities.

One might try to dismiss these devitalising agents as necessary evils of the convenience age. A society dependent upon instant fixes and instant communications, instant satisfactions and instant just about everything. One might, until one realises that they are impregnating and polluting our bloodstream, subtly altering our DNA and changing our very nature from inside out … and from outside in. What kind of insanity is this?

Just witness the tens of thousands of spiky steel mobile phone towers that now cover the Earth like something out of HG Wells' 'War of the Worlds'. Each one spewing its mind-bending unseen microwaves into the surrounding community. And all because everyone has to have a cell phone with which to engage in what, for the majority, are typically banal, bland and boring conversations.

I have written about Transhumanism in preceding chapters, and the plans for a human engineered robotic cyber intelligence to usurp responsibility for the future (and the present) from humankind. I warned that we must be alert to this cold-blooded cybernetic concept gaining ground, especially amongst those who wish to divest themselves of all sense of responsibility for planetary life, and indeed the lives of future generations.

Now I wish us to direct our attentions towards the role that the smartphone addiction is playing in hastening this further demise of homo sapiens. It's a slippage that leads towards an almost wholly derailed human race. One that relies on a machine to do the thinking while the time-honoured neocortex loses its capacity to function; to discern between what is reality and what is virtual reality. What is actual and what is illusory. What is real and what is unreal.

Many is the occasion upon which I have taken my seat on a train and found myself surrounded on all sides by people staring hypnotically into their illuminated smartphones, tablets, iPhones/ iPods, laptops and god knows what else. Tweeting and twittering out endless text messages to social media sites and fellow twittering twots. Watching movies; or just scrolling...scrolling...endlessly scrolling. Which rhymes with 'strolling', but has long since usurped the role of this pleasing outdoor pursuit.

All the while a spreading cloud of electro-smog penetrates corpuscles and brain cells alike, disrupting and distorting the waveforms that constitute the natural channels and interface of communication, between us and indeed between all species

We need a law, following the lines of the 'passive smoker' rebellion, which will outlaw such activities and protect the non-user of wireless technology against brain bending microwaves zapping the unprotected neocortex of unsuspecting neighbours. But it took around forty years of intense lobbying and tens of thousands of 'scientific papers' to prove that smoking cigarettes causes cancer. How long and how many casualties will it take to achieve protection from electromagnetic radiation?

Legislation alone achieves just so much; 'just so little'. There are one thousand and one toxic nasties that should have been legislated against decades ago. Unless society as a whole is moving towards a degree of enlightened awareness, not all the rules in the world are going to alter the underlying problem: the majority of mankind prefers to be a slave rather than to be a leader or responsible partner within the global family of man.

Does it make much difference if one is a slave to a cyborgian dynasty or to an Illuminati empire? Not much, in my view. However, we have at least started a serious awareness-raising 'resistance' to the latter, and know this devil better than we understand the creeping paralysis of virtual reality Transhumanism.

Of course, there are strong links between these two. The ambition has always been to hold the development of humanity in check, by whatever means. He who stands in the shadows between the CEOs of Google, Facebook and Microsoft is a fellow diner at the top table with those who stand in the shadows behind Monsanto, Cargill and Bayer. Who in turn maintain just a shoulder's distance from the shadow conductors of Raytheon's military-industrial project, the Lawrence Livermore Laboratory and British Aerospace Ltd. Who, in their own turn, stand just a stone's throw from the Rockefeller, Rothschild and Soros banking empires.

Each drinking from the others' One World Cup.

Yes, we know something about this. But 'mainstream mortal' knows next to nothing. Yet we share our journey through life with such mortals and cannot turn our backs.

The smartphone is the favourite toy of the non-discerning, as well as too many of the seemingly discerning. Its innocuous nature makes it particularly addictive. Hard to give up, even when you know it's cooking your brain. 'Smart' technologies come to us as an array of seductive weapons ('smart meters' and 'smart cars' are just the beginning) which are clearing the way for the next generation of mind and blood altering 'listening' technologies. Technologies that will, if the cyborgs get their way "do our thinking for us". And, as I have already stated, this is exactly what far too many want and what the control system counts on, in order to spin humanity into the sticky folds of its all-embracing web.

It is this slow road to asphyxiation that particularly alarms me. Each step of the takeover seems 'just a small thing'—on its own, but quickly adds up to a deeply sinister poisoning of the sanctity of life, once observed as the planned interconnected sequence of events that it really is.

The mass indulgence in cybernetics is a fool's game. It's a powerful distraction from the real task facing humanity: the discovery and realisation of our still largely untapped deeper powers of love, spirit and passion. These are the qualities that will define any future worth living in, not an obsession with high-tech wizardry placed on the global market by the cold, calculating minds that drive the multinational behemoths.

Yet even as I write there is emerging another irresistible sweetener to take the cyber-slaves into their ultimate virtual reality scam: WiFi 'Cloud Technology'. A grid of all-encompassing energetic WiFi microwave bands loaded with smart meter intelligence gathering capabilities and a virtually limitless range of capacity available to all who buy in to its ubiquitous Eye of Horus network.

A sub-reality world which is able to declare itself 'the new reality' by dint of its calculated hold over billions who have long since given themselves over to 'the Network'. A network essential to the successful establishment of a One World Control System.

So here we are, ladies and gentlemen. The message "sent from my iPod" might now offer a little jolt to anyone who is taking this seriously. If not, am I (as the owner of a PC but no mobile) to expect "I'm a Cloud supporter" to appear on colleagues' incoming email messages in the near future?

Where is the resistance going to come from if the tools of resistance are all made by the architects of the apocalypse?

How will people know when to abandon their cybernetic ship before it completely devours them?

Are our innards to be sacrificed to genetic engineering and our brains to transhumanist madmen?

Not as long as one remains a proud and resilient human being on this sacred planet Earth. Not as long as enough of us seize this critical moment and declare our commitment to beauty, spontaneity and creativity. Not as long as we stand for truth, thus shattering the malevolent lies of those drugged and soulless automatons who wish to drag us down into their bland metallic graves.

Onward, questing souls. Dispense with these toxic tools of fashion; unsheathe instead the fine tipped arrows of truth—then step forth bravely—for ours is the hour!

Sedation by soundbite

Millions upon millions of educated, and even 'aware' people, all over the world, are succumbing to a new virus 'SBS', or 'SoundBite Syndrome'. Its symptoms are best described as an inability to concentrate on anything meaningful for more than a very short period of time.

To concentrate the mind so as to read something that requires a certain depth of thought or fuller cognisance, is becoming an endangered skill.

Now that is a truly shocking fact. One that should register high on the shocking fact ratio. It should jolt us all into recalling the vital role that genuine communication plays in the passing of essential knowledge and inspiration, including lyrical poetry and vivid prose.

For these great tools of consciousness raising to be corrupted into a thousand broken pieces of easily assimilated soundbites, must constitute one of the most masterful silent weapons of destruction of our oppressor's war chest.

It's not just the children who grow up on a diet of sugary sweets, synthetic colouring agents and indigestible preservatives who can't concentrate on their school work; there are now great swaths of the population as a whole who need to have their reading matter served up to them in the same manner as a fast food outlet doles out its instant processed meals.

What this does, is to put all the most valuable writings, be they literary, spiritual, historical or even scientific, out of reach of what amounts to the best part of an entire generation, particularly those growing up in the instant access era. Those who have become so pap fed with processed communication bites that their brains have shrunk. In such cases, certain regions of the neocortex, lacking stimulation and activity over an extended period of time, become virtually dead zones.

Thus the attention span required to absorb and reflect on a decent analytical video, a thoughtful blog or a great work of literature, is literally inaccessible to exactly those who need it the most. This plays into the hands of the fabricators of spin and slick advertising. It means that many remember an advert slogan more easily than that which is going on either side of it. SoundBite Syndrome, or 'attention deficit disorder' as it is known in the trade, is a disease ruthlessly exploited by corporate media exponents in all post-industrial cultures.

Tragically, it is the innocent minds of young children that are most easily infected. Dumped in front of the TV, video or game app by their distracted parents, they quickly absorb the tailored mind-controlling ingredients on display. And it is questionable whether, after a number of years of this torture, they can ever fully recover the innocence of imagination that is crucial to the development of independent thought and creativity in later life.

Sedation by soundbite is, in particular, the superficial hallmark of much social media text messaging and aptly named 'tweeting' and 'twittering'. Too many are tweeting, twittering and frittering away their lives in cul-de-sacs of banal banter; and in the process, degrading an entire culture of mind skills that once led to thoughtful, careful and reflective communication. That which draws upon the well of human insight and applies it with specific intent in order to convey the deeper emotions and concerns we all need to shape and share, every day of our lives.

The ever-quickening pace of life in the 'profession conscious' fast lane of today's status quo is a subliminal death trap. The slower reflective process, which would ultimately temper and counteract the ever smaller and faster subdivisions of time that typify the ambitious socialite, are systematically pushed to one side by an essentially fragmented, adrenalin-driven lifestyles.

The commitment to deep thought and a mulling-over of the pros and cons of what one is engaged in, are seen as an unnecessary intrusion on the all-important work and play ethos. An ethos, that when analysed, turns out to be the slave's indoctrination commitment to his/her master. The master, in most cases, being 'the establishment'; the 0.5% who form the capstone of the power pyramid that runs the planet. The establishment which acts as the master control unit whose empires expand in direct proportion to the degree to which the human brain of the rest of humanity, shrinks.

It is particularly the children who become the sacrificial lambs in this modern day slaughterhouse. And the parents, who thought their children were just nice little playthings to keep them amused between various career options, they are simply the victims of their own blinkered vanities, of their unquestioned and selfserving ambitions. Irrevocably snared by the status quo, they actually believe themselves to be free!

Let us all beware. At almost any time any one of us can fall into this trap. If we have developed sufficient staying power on the road of consciousness, we can usually extract ourselves from this entanglement without too much damage, but few have fully overcome its seductive tentacles.

We need to be ever watchful, not just for ourselves and our children, but for those close to us whom we witness falling. And this is tricky, because no one who believes herself or himself to be free likes being told that they are not, however subtly it is put. We need to guard our sacred language skills and give them their proper due. "In the beginning was the word" —and even if it wasn't—there is no doubt about the sacred nature of the word. There is no doubt about the extraordinary power (for good and evil) of the word.

Neither is there any doubt about the corruptibility of the word. And here one has to include death by subtle emission. Words, once normal parts of a colourful vernacular, go missing. They fail to appear on internet dictionaries; then in ordinary ones. They appear in red on the computer spell check.

Before you know it, the entire foundation of centuries of language wealth is corrupted and undermined. And then, one day, all that will remain in common use will be a clone like replica: George Orwell's 'newspeak'. Let that day never be. For we are as good as dead the day our words become simply the soulless and sterile symbols of banality.

Let us value that which has value and discard that which hasn't. Be careful, even with trivialities as 'R.U.OK?', 'Thanx' and 'gr8'. If we are seduced into a two-tier communication system for ease, convenience, speed, or whatever, we too may be complicit in degrading the deeper powers of communication which are our special gift.

We too risk becoming party to our oppressors' grand ambition to devalue all values and to sterilise, neuter and divide into sound- and 'read-bites' that which is profound, sensual, spiritually vital—and essentially indivisible.

We need to remember that all things sacred can only retain their sacred qualities when they are nurtured, honed and honoured on a daily basis. This requires the application of a certain sobriety and gravitas—an anchoring of the soul.

Tweeting our way to oblivion

People behaving like birds should mark a step forward in the evolutionary capacity of the human race. After all, birds sing melodiously at dawn and dusk, swoop majestically in the open sky and build their nests using only their beaks. I doubt that most humans could build such nests even using two hands.

Do we dulled and listless nine to fivers dance through the streets and burst into rapturous song each dawn and dusk? No, no, not we measured and mannered mortals. Our typical daily response to the circadian rhythms of this universe is to reach into our pockets for a mass-produced electronically energised plastic gizmo, upon which to twitter, tweet and text profound messages to our friends, such as: "what ya doin' this p.m? I'm nackered – need a drink – how about Soho Brasserie around 7 tonight? Hey— saw jamie this mornin'—wow he looked wicked! Let his hair grow out and was sporting Nike lace-ups!" It's a seriously retarded and poor imitation of the birds' version—isn't it?

If only people could pause long enough to actually listen to the song of the birds, maybe even to marvel at their spontaneous and often balletic flight; or simply peer at one of their nests and reflect on its extraordinary design. But no "No time for that—I never look up—too busy." The very same reason given for never seeing the poisoned aerosol ploughing of the very sky in which the birds perform their ritual dances. What a telling indictment of the current inhuman condition of modern man.

When we pass, and our spirit transitions to the next domain, there is, I believe, a timeless illuminated kind of moment when we get to see the full picture of how we used our time here on Earth. At our point of transition, we are, if you like, presented with the results of the exam called life: the accumulated contribution—or lack of contribution—that we made to this Universe in the course of manifesting our earthly existence.

In that timeless space beyond physical life and yet before becoming (once again) pure spirit, we are perhaps confronted by that which we really are; the human expression of that immeasurable gift of life which we each carried with us into this world as children; as unconscious, yet supremely potent glassy-eyed little Godheads, emerging out of the fecund mother womb. Then, as we grow, carrying forward and nurturing, as best we can, this seed of our limitless potentiality. And ultimately, at that moment of passing, our accumulated earthly truths have their unconditional confrontation with Universal Truth.

At this moment 'wasted time' measures up against purposefully utilised time, and whichever swings the scales its way decides our soul's further progression or regression in the life to come. The positive actions that contributed to the furtherance of the creative potential with which we started this adventure, will lift us higher on our ongoing journey— all that which encourages the furtherance of the evolution of this planet into a consciously loving and creative force for the better.

But the first signposts of our initiation appear when we are yet young. For it is then when we first notice the big divisions in the road ahead and have the task of choosing, or not choosing, to follow the calling of our hearts and our expectant soul. A task which further tests us as we become young adults and gain greater awareness of the contradictions presented by a world at war (with itself) and the ever-present potential within each of us to change that condition into its opposite.

That is our 'exam paper'. Forget the stuff that's called 'exams' which we are forced to grapple with in secondary school. They are the distorted and entombed version of the real thing. They are simply a way of bypassing our true rite of passage. A bypass built by those carrying an ulterior motive: the intention of making sure that we never get the priceless opportunity to stand face to face with our own destiny at a moment when the great majority of our life stands still ahead of us.

It is a deliberate and coldly inhuman calculation, designed to harness the majority of mankind to the yoke of unquestioned slavery to the matrix. And if successful, it ensures that a vast swath of humanity will be tied up in the nine to five sterile work ethics for a good part of the rest of their days. A process that also has the effect of holding back the greater evolution of planetary awareness as a whole.

Of course, there is no telling which side of the line those who do succeed in facing their rite of passage will fall. The road of life, even within the confines of the status quo, is not without its twists and turns. Yet opportunities to get onto our true paths are always present, but remain veiled and often disguised by the distractions of the absurd and power-hungry paraphernalia of modern living. So it is that symbolically or actually, much of the 'civilised' world is tweeting and twittering its way to oblivion.

And when that day of oblivion finally draws close at hand and its cool breath is felt on the nape of the neck, it will be understood that all earlier attempts to put off the honestly confronting and reflecting upon the meaning of life—and the great passing— amounted to a futile and tragically wasteful disregard of our best human energies. The 'judgment day' as it is historically known, cannot be anesthetised. It cannot be erased from existence by our wrapping ourselves up in empty discourses and the fashionable superficial banter of our time.

In the end, this is just a way of trying to hide our fear of embracing the bigger life to which our starved souls are directing us. So to all those bent forward, squinting over their plastic pocket sized electronically enlivened screens, or chatting uselessly on their microwave cell phones, only to then go home to spend the rest of their evening in front of the mind control screen on the living room wall—I want to say: we have no right to kill the spirit with which we were and are so richly endowed. In the highest spiritual circles, committing suicide is considered a great irreverence and a major karmic burden in lives to come.

More than this even, it is an act of abandonment of our responsibility to take charge of our destinies and make something out of them. To give back to that creative source which gave us life something more than that with which we started. For example, some fine individual expression of our gratitude to our Creator.

It is the growth of manifest spirit which is the true growth in us humans: the increase we make in the number and quality of dancing reflective prisms in the diamond of Life.

From the pure unconscious of the child to the forged and sculptured consciousness of the adult—that is our life work.

The preoccupation with 'economic growth' is a subconscious and sublimated compensation for a lack of expansion of the spirit and the soul of man; the growth of the divine human which is our true reason to be. Power, politics and a preoccupation with acquiring material possessions, is the expression of life gone off course. Of submission to our oppressors' plan for humanity's slavery.

So if you still insist in twittering away your life—at least twitter something meaningful like: "I'm seeing the sun, renewed, blazing forth as it climbs into the vastness of the morning sky. I feel my soul expanding... I feel like soaring as a bird soars, leaping like gazelle leaps. Today I'm in celebration of life! I'm arranging a meeting with the calling of my destiny—I'm throwing off the shackles of meaningless repression, dear friend, how about you?" Tweet your way to heaven that way—or don't tweet at all.

Leave it to the birds. For they, at least, only know to communicate in poetry.

Raising the Spirit

The subjugation of the Creator

Have you ever reflected on what might be the ultimate goal of the oppressors of humanity? I have—and this is what emerged.

Those in pursuit of power are seldom satisfied. They always want more. In a seemingly never-ending act of compulsive consumption, they seek to dominate or destroy all that stands in the way of their thirst for power.

The forces that currently hold a controlling influence over this world are of this stable. Their goal of 'full spectrum dominance' or 'total domination' of various aspects of this planet is not the summation of their ambition, it is a mere stepping-stone along the way.

On the way to what?

On the way to becoming masters of the Universe.

The macrocosm has a dual energetic essence: an evolving outward force and an imploding inward force. An iridescence of light and an impenetrable darkness. A blazing sun and a black hole. Multiple members of each of course.

This theme of duality plays out throughout the macrocosm and microcosm—through the totality of life. Through sentient and insentient matter; down to the neutron, electron, cells, molecules, atoms and sub atomic particles.

Everywhere energy is dual. Electricity requires the interaction and clash between opposing forces in order to be that highly energetic element that it is.

While the evolution of the plant and animal kingdom is clearly attracted and aligned to the vibratory waves of the Creator, man has a choice: the choice to follow the call of the soul—or the choice not to follow the call of the soul. To evolve or to slide into entropy. This makes man a pretty unique species.

When we examine ourselves, we find that we have a duality of choice in all we say and do, at all times. There is a continual clash here. The friction which results from this clash provides propulsion. A propulsion, which, like the plant kingdom, aspires to the light. But only if we are true to our calling.

Constantly catching our attention are a host of signposts drawing us towards various routes that divert us from our true calling, each promising much in the way of material wealth, ego satisfying power and physical convenience.

The net worth of our life depends upon which of the two fundamental roads we elect as the predominant influence. Which of these two pulls we make our main priority. The innately divine voice of our intuition or the ulterior motive, materialistic attraction? There is a third: the fear-based 'safety' route.

In the course of our exploration and recognition of the degrading elements of life (in ourselves) we come across many symptoms of the ulterior motive. Irrational cravings that tend to obscure and weigh down our ability to respond to the call of higher truth; to the signals of the soul.

Due to the afflictions that have long dominated the human race, we are born into a world predominantly governed by manifestations of these crass, misdirected motives.

One such is the desire for a type of power which gives the illusion of being greater, or at least more alluring, than our still subtle innately divine intuitive power.

This ego-fuelled power has ample room to develop because our subtle innate power is realised and takes form, only gradually. We thus cannot avoid spending considerable amounts of time under the influence of that which is the antithesis of the call to the light. In spite of the fact that this antithesis is, in effect, an abstraction. A virtual reality. The condition this present world suffers under 24/7.

Carlos Castaneda, author of The Teachings of Don Juan and many other titles, refers to this condition as 'the foreign installation'.

If we allow ourselves, we who were gifted 'freedom of choice', to take this abstract road towards a power which appears greater than our slowly unfolding innate natural power, we will find that it is a road well-travelled. So well-travelled in fact, that it gives the impression of being the only road we can take, especially since the great majority of people we know are on it.

Not only this, in choosing to pursue further a journey that is at odds with the pull of our souls, we soon come across guides, figureheads and high priests, all of whom are only too willing to soften our passage and further pacify our inner being. Keep going, and doctors of darkness emerge who will enable the traveler of this road to gain new powers and skills to further aid his/her wilful ambitions.

Such skills enable the initiate to start practising, in daily life, a kind of subliminal black magic. The power to 'get one's way' in all one does. To take possession of that which one wishes to possess. To become well-adjusted to the darkness and ever more in denial of the light. Ultimately landing up as obedient servants to the dark side hierarchy.

To fully give one's self over to 'the foreign installation' is to follow a reverse sequence for humankind. Symbolised by the Nazi Swastika, a reversed ancient symbol of peace and one of the main tools of those in service to their dark masters.

Most who dabble in the dark side's satanic pilgrimage don't ever get to the inner sanctum, fortunately. However, they do themselves (and others) a great deal of harm along the way. But those that do get an open door to the inner sanctum, become the chosen purveyors of a reversed logic for the planet. Such people manifest themselves wherever positions of insentient hierarchical power and control are dominant.

In this reversed world, our innate divinity is turned inside out, becoming a near total immersion into atheistic narcissism: the mark of the beast—one of whose more blatant manifestations is our rampant consumer society.

Carried to its nadir, the pursuit of power takes the form of a total consumption of the all; the complete subjugation of the Creator and replacement with a false idol that takes on the characteristics of a god in its own right. The abstract, insentient god of disenfranchised divine power.

It is this alien hybrid that seeded its way onto an innocent Earth in ages past, stealing the gold from an unsullied Eden.

The end game of our tormentors has always been to possess this blessed planet and suck from it all vestiges of love, passion and compassion. Because they provide the fuel for the process whereby the dark omega point can be reached; the divine universe conquered, to be replaced by a virtual reality Transhuman sham.

This is the world entered into by any being who freely elects to follow the calling of the 'foreign installation' instead of the Supreme Creator.

Duality has no 'no man's land' middle ground. Not to be on the path of truth is to be on the path of untruth; and unless corrected (and there are ample opportunities for correction) this road ends in a black hole.

For those who fully embrace a march to the black hole, the world is not enough. For the eternal craver of power, and those driven by a deep fear of the unknown, only the possession of the entire universe seems likely to satiate their inner emptiness.

However, that seemingly unquenchable appetite will never get its craved for satiation, as what such entities do not fully comprehend, is that all attempts to subjugate the

Creator must ultimately prove futile. For the very act of trying triggers—somewhere deep in the universe—an opposite movement. The rebirth of life-light. A counterpoint that cannot be constrained.

As this force grows in intensity, we sense our own rebirth quickening. Not just this, but also that the poisoned protagonists of darkness, for all their brazen arrogance, are trembling.

We who press onwards, confronting the seemingly impenetrable grip that our tormentors hold over us, burn inside with an unquenchable passion for fulfilment of our quest. This passion is transformative. It brings us to our Omega Point. The exact opposite of the dark side's entropic end game.

Here, at our Omega Point, we find ourselves offering our full support for this great Universe that bore us in the first place. We burst with the love we long to share, to give back. To honour our Creator.

And it is here, in this quintessential moment, that our Creator witnesses that which He Is – and we – that which We Are. And we are the same.

Fully conjoined in a Oneness that disguises the duality which brought it into being.

Concerning the integration of past experiences

Nothing which becomes manifest ever disappears. It becomes integrated into the great body of ethereal matter we call 'the collective unconscious.'

If we try to sublimate our painful and less happy experiences, they will simply reappear at our time of passing, and play their role in determining the work still required of us in the next cycle of reincarnation.

But we can lay all before the omnipotent compassion of Source and ask to be aided in our process of psychic and emotional healing. Healing and integration are two indivisible parts of one whole.

Pushing away that which we feel disinclined to face up to actually makes that thing stronger. It's an interesting irony. But once we accept that we have to take responsibility for our actions—all of them—then we start the process of defeating the demon at our door.

It's a process which responds positively (not unlike our digestive systems) when what we choose to 'take in' is in harmony with that which is good, fair, honest and healing. If we deem ourselves superior (or inferior) to such a commitment, and pursue a path of self-acclimation and/or shallow conformity with the trends of the day, then only trouble awaits us as the passage of life unfolds. Neither is it about attempting to nullify and demolish ego.

We all need some ego, but in correct proportions. Abolish ego altogether, and you will find yourself stranded in a world which largely operates according to ego centered principles, and will have only yourself to hold responsible for your demise.

It has always been and will always be, about balance. Balance is the art of living. The Art of Living.

Now the balance to which I refer is not about refusing to take a moral position while sitting on the fence in the middle of a field, where on one side GM crops are being planted and on the other organic farming is in progress. That, of course, is the opposite of balance. Failure to act when faced by obvious wrong is in the end a criminal act.

I chose the famous statement by Einstein to head the introduction to my book 'Changing Course for Life' "The world is a dangerous place, not because of those who do evil, but because of those who look on and do nothing." A profoundly true judgement.

The real balance that we aim for in our daily lives involves weighing up the contents of each predicament which confronts us, and arriving at a solution which provides the most positive outcome possible.

Now this cannot be achieved without actively engaging in the deliberate use of lateral, holistic thinking. We have this problem or challenge right up ahead—it seems to stymie us—no obvious answer as to how to overcome it. Yet, shift the whole thing into a broader more universal context, stand back and look at it anew, and suddenly a solution presents itself.

Balance is a dynamic thing. It involves seizing hold of something, engaging it in a very direct way and then walking the tightrope wire which passes right down its middle, metamorphosing it into that which is no longer a problem, but a creative and positive act of transformation and change.

Yes, my friends, that is indeed the Art of living. There is absolutely nothing we cannot achieve once possessed of this skill. And it is a skill. Like all things wise and wonderful, one must beaver away at the material one has in hand in order to mold it into a thing of beauty and resonance. Nothing great comes without pursuing it with conscious, sustained effort, in this third density existence.

So it is with the integration of our past experiences. That which haunts us from our past will fail to spook us any longer, provided we decide to go at it in the spirit of a valuable challenge. To say to ourselves "OK, I mucked that one up big time, but actually I now see that the actions I took were the ones I decided upon out of my own free will. Perhaps I needed to go through this experience owing to some necessary learning curve without which I would not have had the chance to recognise some vital home truths. And I begin to see, that it is in fact these truths that enable me to now go forward and to become freed of old phobias." I am not referring to early childhood years, as in those years we are not in a position to take a controlling position over our lives.

Turning that which is perceived as a block into that which becomes the opposite is one of the most life affirmative experiences one will ever have. And once one has got started, there is no reason why there should not be an infinite number of such transformations during our lifetimes. We are, after all, blessed with infinite consciousness, but cannot know this until at least some element of it becomes manifest. And it won't become manifest except by squaring up to the challenges that life presents us.

So those who are currently going through the mill, take heart, your oppressor may well turn out to be the source of your salvation.

Many describe how the source of their pain and confusion comes from childhood experiences. There is a tendency to blame our parents for our own shortcomings. To see one's self as crippled by the circumstances of one's early years and to fall victim to the notion that one can't overcome these shortcomings.

But in truth, this is not so. It is not mere whimsy to suggest that we may well choose the circumstances of our birth. That, as I described above, we landed up where we needed to land up in order to have another chance to successfully overcome previous unmet challenges. We have many chances to redeem ourselves in the greater scheme of things.

It is the nature of cosmic Lila to eternally offer the chance to each of us to overcome our weaknesses and progress on the beckoning road of conscious awareness. But no one, except a poser, has suggested it will be an easy ride, laid out for us on a silken road of love and light.

We have 'free will'. It is, I believe, a contract that the Supreme made with man right from the beginning. We were given all the means required to make our lives into that which resonates with divine exigence. Our Creator will not interfere or intervene in doing this job for us. Not even if one prays from sunset to sundown for his intervention.

But he will make it known that he resides within every being who seeks him. And that one can and will be guided on one's chosen path, so long as one is sincere, is drawn by the magnet of truth and is able to calm oneself enough to listen, and respond, to the voice of intuition.

Conditional upon following this course, is to find it in one's self to honor one's parents. Even when they have caused us to suffer. Because they themselves no doubt suffered because of the shortcomings of their childhood—and so on into the past—ad infinitum. The great majority most probably knew no better than to dictate the terms of parenthood that they felt to be the most fitting in their time.

We do both them and ourselves a disservice by failing to free ourselves from the resentment that often surrounds a dystopian upbringing. The true integration of past experiences starts with dropping the old baggage and breathing a great sigh of relief at having done so. However, I do recognise that in some particularly harsh childhood circumstances, the scars may take a long time to heal. Even a lifetime.

This does not negate the fact that everything we do and have experienced in our lives remains with us; but once we have come to terms with our greatest difficulties, that which has weighed us down slowly takes a back seat, fading into the background. The pain can't simply be wished away; but it can be quietly and profoundly accepted and integrated into our ongoing evolution towards true awareness. So done, it will no longer bother us. Compassion will fill that void.

Then we can set sail on our adventure, freed from the deadweight of our old, self-imposed, false beliefs. An adventure in which we alone are at the helm. An adventure which will make or break us—and if it breaks us it is because that is what was needed to continue onwards. Be brave.

The great turning

Autumn is a wonderful season especially for those sensitive to the pulls exerted by the Earth's core.

That means those ready to be pulled downwards. Those who do not resist the binding of all disparate energies recalled to the source during 'The Fall'. Here is where we find ourselves again. In awe to this great recurring gravitational episode of life.

The Equinox is upon us—and 'fall' we must. Along with the browned and sunburned leaves that flutter to nature's floor. Along with the retreating earthworms, bees and the last windblown butterflies of summer.

For it is only when we too allow ourselves to fall that we can experience the full power of the great turning and be refuelled and refreshed, made ready for a renewed rising when the sun once again spreads its waxing powers upon a receptive planet.

Of all the seasons, this is the most important one not to be rushed in. Autumn is nature's resting and restoring ground—it is her meditation. Go in, in, in, and see for yourself what treasures there are! What mysteries hang in the softly rising mist that lays a protective shroud over the mantle of this Earth.

Give yourself the rest you need. The contemplation. Do not deny yourself the 'letting go' that nature teaches. Do not make excuses for why you can't re-find the you whom you really are. Do not fight the essential repose that is at the heart of autumn. At the heart of 'the fall'. For if we will not fall how can we arise again? Do not let the flattened landscape of military-industrial havoc take your soul instead.

This is the message of the great turning—and we humans are a part of it. We are 'of nature'. That is what we fight for when we go out to do battle with the mad destroyers. This is why we give our all to block the GMO, the 'fracking', the nuclear madness—all the toxic killers. Somewhere within us we remain at one with the great circadian rhythm of the seasons. The trouble is, that 'somewhere' is (for most) buried under a great pile of superficial, superfluous paraphernalia that swamps nature's messenger, blocking all attempts to receive the call we are meant to hear.

Such a garbage-laden blockage prevents us from deepening our emotional being; so much so that we can no longer draw from the well of life. We cannot be renewed, enriched and readied for what is to come. The autumn just passes— and is herself saddened by the lack of company on her ongoing journey towards the winter solstice.

A saddened nature is less resistant to combating the toxic insanities which are dumped upon her. Her immune system is weakened, and in this state that which kills, kills more readily. While we kill nature, she is trying to live. She is reminding us, every minute of every day, that we should also live. She never tires in this.

That, maybe, is the reason why those who can't stop to listen would rather put an end to her. Put an end to that persistent voice that has an annoying habit of reminding us that there is something altogether wrong with the way we are living our lives and the way we treat that which nourishes us.

To many, the answer to this nagging interruption to their daily addictions is to shoot the messenger. No gun required; just turn on the TV, crack open a beer, go to the fridge, stick on a catchy piece of music; chat on the internet, mow the lawn, fiddle with the smartphone— you know the rest.

Then there's another way of shooting the messenger: get a job which negatively impacts upon the health and welfare of this living, breathing planet. That means most jobs. Because most 'jobs' are built upon a denial that the great turning even exists! They plough right through and flatten it without even realising it's there. They nullify the life force with their money-obsessed paralysis, thus rendering void all things living.

'Nine to five' is not the way to stay alive; it is a programmed parasitic work ethic designed to automate and suck the life out of humanity. Avoid this fate if you want to remain sentient and subtle enough to respond to the messenger's call.

Now, as the northern light draws in once again; as the sun's rays soften their summer brightness turning to amber hues of golden warmth—go with them. Even if it pelts with rain—splash with it.

Go to the fecund underworld which quietly ferments that which has passed and slowly rekindles the sleeping seed that is the new life to come. Go there. For this journey is life's gift and it is madness not to dip deeply into so potent a brew.

Our world stands on the brink of discovering itself anew. We are a ripening fruit on the tree of life. The great change that we yearn for awaits within us to be given clearance to fly. You have only to let go of your hold on that which holds no promise.

Let all things superficial fall away. Let gravity take them to be melted down in the great furnace below. Let all become deep and move to the rhythm of celestial callings. Remove the watch whose hands tick off the hours—telling only the story of linear time and the division of oneness into a million splintered parts. Nano particles that glitter in the neon flattering windows of sterile main street money. Let die that part of you which still clings to such a nefarious chimera.

A great turning is upon us. Spare this day to enter its temple. Touch a deeper seam in your trembling soul and share your treasure joyfully. Do not deny yourself the initiation and rite of passage that awaits you. For what emerges out again from here will bring to our war-torn world a profoundly needed nourishment.

Seizing control of our destinies

In 1381, at a time of great repression for the British agricultural work force, an extraordinary people's revolutionary named Wat Tyler sprang to his feet and announced "England should be a nation of self-governing communities" to which he added "No lord shall exercise lordship over the people, and, as we are oppressed by so vast a hoard of bishops and clerks, the property of the holy church should be taken and divided."

His colleague, the priest John Ball, spoke out with equal fervour "The lords' claims to be more lords than we are rest solely on their power to force us to labour that they may spend."

A great surge of support for these proclamations swept through the farming communities of South East England, quickly spreading further North. The farmers took up arms—whatever appropriate implements they could find in the farmyard—and set out on their mission to free themselves from the wicked landlords and clerks, who between them were taxing the life out of the farming communities throughout the land, destroying the livelihoods of thousands of countryside families.

Many a pernicious bureaucrat was confronted by this motley army, with the brave farmer, Wat Tyler, proudly riding at its head, and many a selfish landlord was forced to concede his greedy rental regime and bow to the demands of the English peasants.

And yes, blood was shed in the struggle to gain respect for basic human rights.

A great quest for liberation, justice and equality blazed amongst the downtrodden land-workers and villagers of fourteenth century England during those famous months of The Peasant's Revolt. Only an act of royal treachery finally stopped this revolution from fully undermining the corrupted power of the State and the intransigence of King Richard II.

Why do I tell this story?

Because more than six hundred years after this peasant uprising shook the nation, we have come full circle. Once again the call is going out for peoples and regions under the hand of oppressive, dictatorial regimes, to become 'self-governing communities'. Wat Tyler's heroic stand echoes down the ages and nourishes the cause of non-compliance and community actions that stand up against the ever more insidious tentacles of centralised power.

Right now there are one hundred and fifty communities in the United States redefining their right to self-govern and pushing forward their programs for localised renewable energy and ecological food security. Not only this, they are also rewriting the laws that govern their communities and declaring citizens' charters, banning GMs and initiating local seed saving actions. They are also declaring the right to clean water and are making 'fracking' a criminal offence.

In the process, through collective acts of civil disobedience, they are stripping the corporate world of its powers. These communities are able to show how the notion that corporations have some form of sovereign power—is just a facade; how it is people who hold sovereign power, as Wat Tyler made plain all those years ago. And it is people who must again exercise that power.

All over the World such stirrings are gaining momentum. Actions to reclaim powers usurped by that toxic cocktail of government and corporate collusion are breaking out. If such stands are being taken in the US heartlands of corporate and government connivance, then it proves that the will of the people is more powerful than the will of the hierarchical cabal whose ambition it is to control all aspects of our lives. We should draw strong inspiration from these game-changing actions—and increase our own determination to go in the same direction.

The time has come for all awakening individuals to hone a definite life strategy. A strategy that puts us in the driver's seat and empowers us to set a new course; one imbued with creative inventiveness, courage and mutual support.

We have arrived here because of the accumulated evidence which overwhelmingly proves that the status quo is a fraud. Designed to strip us of our powers of judgment and the determination to act on that judgment. There is no time for further deliberation of the pros and cons of this or that political polemic. It's all a miasma. A massive sham. A sham which we continue to uphold as long as we go on playing along with its sense of self-importance; giving it a status it does not actually possess, and then sheltering under its poisoned wing.

Every day that goes by without putting into place a strategy to step out of this straightjacket is a day wasted—a sacrificial offering to all that is sucking the life out of humanity.

Self-government starts by taking control of the self. By shaking off the doubts about one's capabilities and taking specific steps to enhance one's powers: spiritually, mentally and physically. We need to be aware that there is no predestined design for this life that will fatalistically play itself out while we bury our heads in the sand.

Yet we are indoctrinated to believe that there is some kind of inevitability in the way the world lurches from crisis to crisis, from war to war. That suits the cabal very well, because it is their war game that is being enacted on planet Earth, and the more people that see that war game as somehow 'inevitable', the longer will it go on desecrating the fabric of life.

Just now, many are falling into the trap of declaring that we are inevitably heading for a Third World War. But in so doing they are merely fulfilling the ambitions of those craven agents of death whose game design includes that scenario. Our role is not to prophecy, but to change the goal posts so as to ensure that such horrors never take place. That is the meaning of 'seizing control of our destiny'.

If, in spite of our efforts, such a war breaks out, it is simply because there is insufficient energy focused on the true path of life. Insufficient self-discipline to steer against the tide of doom. But every person who gives in to a sense of doom when confronted by the machinations of the war machine has failed to grasp the powers with which they are endowed. Powers to change themselves as well as the assumed course of events. Forging a path of truth where presently are deserts of desolation.

Wat Tyler and his gallant peasant followers did not stand back and allow repression to rule. Nor should we. He proclaimed that no hierarchical figure should rule over and repress the people. So should we. He called instead for England to become a nation of self-governing communities. So should we—in whatever Country we reside.

Because this is surely the only practical antidote to the super centralisation of our lives and absolute rule by the despotic fiefdoms of the twenty-first century.

Self-governing communities turn out to be our most instinctual socio-economic model of survival and create the right setting for a fertile organic expansion of the spiritual and artistic path. Because to be 'spiritually aware' 'self- governing' and a 'caring community' are fundamental to the growth of responsible and cohesive shared living. Everything else that poses as a solution is already shot full of holes.

Humanity is an extended family. But as in the present tragedy which is Jew versus Arab, Muslim versus Christian, Israel versus Palestine, this truth has been riven with lies and ripped apart by ulterior motives.

Modern 'democracies' are now simply a perpetually repeating expression of this divide and conquer holocaust. It is impossible to become awake and then continue to put both feet back into such a deeply compromised and incongruous system as we have today. Therefore we must change the script.

Everyone should already be concentrating themselves on the process of building—or contributing to the building of—self-governing communities. Increasingly freed from dependence on the fallen model.

As the foundations of the status quo continue to crack apart, so do the seemingly reliable sources of life dependencies to which we are accustomed also go with them. There is no more time to sit on fences. They are themselves rotting away underneath us and will soon turn to dust.

We who have become 'aware'—are the leaders of the age. We must live up to this reality. We know that the status quo is beyond redemption. So we must take this knowledge to be the signal to build that which will redeem our collective Human status; which will carry us through the apocalypse. We know what the ingredients are that will make our arks self-sustaining. We know what we need in order to come alive again. Now we must put them all together—for that is where they belong.

If we are to overcome that which oppresses us we must unite our creative powers and imaginations in common affirmation of the life force with which we are each endowed.

The quest for liberation, justice and basic equality so nobly fought for by Wat Tyler and the peasant's revolt six hundred years ago, is now our revolution.

The world is our garden

When we walk into a carefully nurtured and diverse garden, we are struck by its beauty and its sense of completeness. We are enraptured by its scents and its mysteries. We are enlivened by its colors, both vivid and subtle, and we are nourished by the freshness that fills our lungs.

Altogether, the majority of sentient beings will surely concur, this garden is a most agreeable place to be, and should someone emerge who threatens to desecrate this sacred space, the reaction will be to jump to its defence and protect it against such a criminal action.

So let us consider the fact that many a wise person and many a spiritual leader has felt impelled to point out that "The World Is Our Garden" and that it should therefore be tended, nurtured and defended in the same way as the private space in which we grow our flowers, fruits, vegetables and herbs. Emotionally, we should make no distinction between these micro and macro spheres.

Yet look around today and what do we see?

Certainly, there are many mortals tending their individual gardens, and many more with no physical garden to tend. But amongst of all these, just a tiny minority can be found who are willing to go out of their way to stand up for that greater garden called planet Earth.

Even amongst those who would class themselves as 'aware' and advancing along the path of enlightenment, one finds too few ready and willing to actively defend the greater whole in the same spirit as they readily defend and tend their 'own' private space. Be that space the place where one cultivates one's spiritual growth or the physical space that is one's own garden.

The act of 'ownership' appears to have overridden and nullified our ability to feel and apply a sense of innate responsibility for that which we don't 'own'.

The neo-liberal capitalist/consumerist conditioning that forms a major part of nearly all our educations, has not taught us to feel responsible for all life, but only that part in which we have invested our personal interest and financial resources.

We need to remind ourselves that we are the collective trustees of this unique living entity that sustains and provides us with all our needs for the duration of our lives—and beyond.

Let us question our supposed 'spirituality' in the light of our unwillingness to lay ourselves on the line to fight for the survival of that which enables us to eat, drink, breathe and take pleasure in its abundant generosity.

You see, if we had been entrained from an early age to respond spontaneously to the life-giving heart-beat of our planetary existence, we would make no distinction between empathy for the garden of Gaia and empathy for our own private garden. Empathy for all children and empathy for our own children ... and so on. We would recognise that the manifestation of our protective instinct to operate only around that which we consider 'belongs to us' is a gross distortion of our natural instincts. Why do I say that? Consider for a moment that you are sitting in your garden and someone comes through the gate with a chain saw and proceeds to set about felling your favourite fruit tree ... what would you do?

Well, you would almost certainly spring up from your chair and rush to stop them. Now let us shift to a similar incident where a beautiful tree in a park on the other side of your garden fence is indiscriminately approached by a man wielding a chain saw who clearly has no business to be there. It is clear that this person intends to cut down this tree ... what would your reaction be to this? Would you try to apprehend this person? Try to find help? Feel a sense of outrage?

There is a chance that you might respond in all these ways; but there is a much greater likelihood that, after experiencing some initial discomfort at the brazenness of this destructive intent, you would take no action, consoling yourself with the thought "There's nothing I can do about it anyway". With that thought uppermost in your mind you would try to ignore the incident and get on with what you were doing.

If our education system had even a smidgen of spiritual aspiration written into its curriculum, we would be encouraged to recognise our responsibility for all life on this planet from an early age, and be encouraged to come to its rescue at times when it is clearly under threat.

But that is not what the majority of schooling is about. On the contrary, it concentrates its energies on teaching us how to acquire the means to 'own' some little niche of this planet, and to accumulate the thousands of bits and pieces that are deemed necessary to furnish it. God forbid that we might decide to reject the trappings of this hallowed road to hell!

Every TV advert, commercial hoarding, glitzy magazine, shop window, internet and cinema screen is imploring us to indulge in a consumptive way of life that both precludes gaining a greater awareness of our predicament, and contributes to the inevitable rape of the planetary resources upon which we all depend.

The rising consciousness that comes with a rising awareness, also has the effect of alerting us to the destructive nature of this consumptive lifestyle and the majority of jobs that constitute the repetitive and largely sterile working week.

We see more and more clearly how, if we are caught in this mechanism, we are just a cog in a vast machine whose overall ambition is precisely the opposite of that which inspires our true endeavors.

It soon becomes obvious that we have to make a choice: find a form of work that satisfies our rising sense of discernment and is supportive of the trusteeship of planet Earth, or give in to the demands and promises of the corporate state that so relentlessly undermines all that is subtle, beautiful and fulfilling in this day- to-day adventure called Life.

The new society so many of us long for can only come about if we take the necessary actions to bring it about. One cannot embark upon a path to higher consciousness while ignoring the damage done through the way one conducts one's daily life. In order to realise our deeper selves and sleeping spiritual powers, we have to bring all aspects of our lives into line with our rising consciousness.

This means embarking upon a disciplined transition away from reliance upon the crude and destructive commercial edifices of the status quo—such as long food miles; profit hungry supermarket chains; highly corrupted large-scale banking institutions; agrichemically and genetically modified 'convenience' foods; unnecessarily large gas-guzzling cars; mind-numbing and mind-controlling TV programs; following 'fashion'; frequent boozing and partying; electro-smog-producing indulgent cell phone conversations … and so on.

Not only are these various pursuits negatively impacting on us and on our surroundings, but by pursuing them we are financially and energetically supporting those facets of society whose sole aim is profit, power and increasing control over our daily lives. In other words, we are supporting that which is part and parcel of the destruction of this 'world that is our garden'.

This is clearly a thoroughly unpropitious path to tread.

We are either supporting a radical transformation of society in line with our own rising awareness of its multiple destructive components, or we are falling into a hypocritical and delusional state in which any gain in awareness is soon undone and turned in upon itself.

We have no choice other than to walk forward on two feet. To 'walk the walk' and to practice what we preach.

It is my belief that we will succeed in this great quest once we have securely tethered our inner awakening to the manifestation of its true outward expression.

Thus the road to enlightenment becomes synonymous with taking actions to ameliorate and heal the social, cultural, economic and environmental scars that cover our wounded planet. A process which unifies otherwise disparate endeavours and reveals disengaged, inward looking and passive practices that shun active participation in service of the planet—to be ultimately fraudulent and a mechanism for escapism.

If 'The World is our garden' then let us be united now in going to rescue it from its enemies – no matter what the odds. Let us defy the political gamesmanship that has led governments to ally with the corporate cause and ignore the cries of imprisoned humanity and the tortured limbs of Mother Nature.

Our highest calling is to come out in defence of life. The angels will rush to our side once we have demonstrated our commitment to taking control of our destinies, which includes the emancipation of this long-oppressed planet which is our unique and irreplaceable home.

Politics of Deception

European superstate – one step closer or imminent collapse?

Jean Monnet, the founding father of the European Union, had a very particular vision of Europe's future back in 1952, and he is purported to have expressed it in a letter to a colleague on 30th April that year:

"Europe's nations should be guided towards the superstate without their people understanding what is happening. This can be accomplished by successive steps, each disguised as having an economic purpose, but which will eventually and irreversibly lead to federation."

Here, in a nutshell, we plainly see the trickery that stands behind the fabricated 'Union' of individual nations, each of which was led to believe that its economic and social stability would prosper once it committed itself to the 'common market' and the various treaties which mark its inexorable passage to 'superstate'. The actual mission of the founders of the EU has always been something of a chimera; Monnet's letter makes it clear however, that the motivation was both idealistic and elitist. The supranational entity was to be created "without (their) people understanding what was happening" following a pattern of elitist oligarchical ambition stretching back through past dynasties.

※ We can trace the roots of this latest 'superstate' experiment to the Schuman Plan of 1951, which was signed up to by six Countries and took the form of a treaty (The Treaty of Paris) centred around coal and steel industries being placed under common management, ostensibly to prevent any recurrence of the death and destruction of the Second World War. Germany, France, Italy, the Netherlands, Belgium and Luxembourg were the signatories to this treaty whose empirical purpose was stated to be ensuring that none of these Countries could ever again manufacture weapons of war to be used against the other.

Then in 1957, the same six Countries expanded cooperation to other economic sectors and signed The Treaty of Rome. Thus creating the 'European Economic Community', also known as The Common Market.

The UK joined up to this in 1973 under the then Prime Minister Edward Heath.

The formal creation of the European Union, under the guidance of Jacques Delors, didn't occur until February 1992 under the Maastricht Treaty. It formalised the introduction of the European Parliament and European Commission, the latter gaining considerable 'management power' under Jacques Santer, its first president. Interestingly the Commission was originally to be named "The High Authority", which has strongly Masonic overtones. But this name was dropped in the 1960s.

※ The single currency (Euro) element of the expanding Union was launched in 1999, along with the European Central Bank. Lastly came the Lisbon Treaty of December 2009 which created the new post of President of the European Council.

Within this brief synopsis of the EU's birth and expansion, we can detect the process of creeping homogenisation which reflects Jean Monnet's covert master plan. As intended, on the surface it certainly appears that economic considerations were to the fore, notwithstanding the supposedly benign 'common' interests like modernised infrastructure, the Common Agricultural Policy and the 'no border' agreements which were deemed to give the EU a more flowing socio-economic (and cultural) connectivity.

The Common Agricultural Policy (CAP) was supposed to ensure that no one would go hungry in the new Europe and that farming interests would be financially protected against undue volatility within the wider market. Needless to say, the subsidised mono crops and intensive livestock holdings of the CAP have proved an unmitigated disaster for traditional bio-diverse mixed family farms, food quality and the ecology of European farmland. Distorted (subsidised) trading policies have also exacted their toll on others.

What is undeniable in all this, is that Monnet's grand experiment has concentrated a very large amount of power into very few hands; and those hands are a long way removed from the hands of the laborers and workers who continue to form the majority of European Union citizens.

The creation of the single currency (Eurozone) has served to expose the fault lines that have, on more than one occasion, come to the surface of EU affairs. Whatever the founding fathers may have thought, the idea that Countries as socially, culturally and economically contrasting as Greece and Germany, could find commonality via some form of 'fiscal agreement' was anything but wise.

The creation of the European Central Bank epitomises the 'trading bloc' mentality of the Eurozone. It has, as Winston Churchill once noted, brought home the fact that the EU could operate like "A United States of Europe". A United States of Europe is just what Europe is becoming, with the president of the European Commission acting as the front man; a powerful central bank acting as Europe's vault, and a weak parliament struggling to introduce some semblance of democracy.

Within this top-heavy and highly bureaucratic regime, global banking cartels have fully exploited the underlying sense of political insecurity. The European Central Bank has teamed up with the International Monetary Fund to act as central controllers of the destinies of struggling Eurozone Countries. The result is a cold and soulless brand of exploitation which appears blind to anything other than the imposition of Orwellian authoritative control structures that suck dry the assets of any Country foolish enough to seek its financial support.

After presiding over the collapse of various European economies, José Manuel Barroso has used his position as President of the European Commission to recommend the imposition of a European Superstate as the only effective medicine left to hold the troubled 'Union' together. Resistance to this solution is taken as an infringement of the spirit of the project and those who dare to raise their voices as 'deniers'. Sixty years on from the date of the Monnet letter the framework of the envisioned superstate is pushed into place.

As ailing Eurozone member states pledge their dwindling national assets to the voracious demands of the IMF and ECB, the interest payments that the IMF and ECB exact continue to fuel the financier led cabal's war chest. Countries outside the Eurozone are now being asked to further top-up this chest, because apparently there is not enough in it to prepare further poisoned loan packages for the next victims.

What Jean Monnet had in mind when he wrote his infamous letter, was the carefully crafted, covert instigation of an ultimate power heist. A heist which firmly installs a small band of all-powerful technocrats and oligarchs in the undisputed driving seat of the largest trading bloc of the planet. Under this regime, the sovereignty of nation states becomes strategically weakened and so heavily dependent upon outside economic support that it ultimately ceases to operate as a functional 'sovereign' system. Decisions of national importance, once made via elected parliaments, are usurped by the centralised control system based in Brussels, but directly linked to London, New York, Washington, Frankfurt, Paris, Rome and Tokyo.

Any Country not part of this 'club' automatically becomes sidelined as a second class nation with little or no right to sit on key committees and influence the future. The fiscal union club is held up as the holy grail by which all nations must abide if they are to be members of the inner sanctum.

Under this regime transnational corporations, bankers and EU bureaucrats flourish, while the working citizens of the EU are imprisoned in a modern serfdom in which the banker-controlled European Commission and signed-up nation states demand that the European labor force bail out the private banks by accepting lower pay, later retirement and the loss of social services.

In this way, we (the people) are asked to carry the can and submit to the austerity measures imposed upon us in order that governments can bail out banks, and banks can satisfy their Eurocrat paymasters ensconced behind their mahogany desks at the European Financial Stability agency. In close proximity also sit the shadowy 'Frankfurt Group'. According to Larry Elliot, economics correspondent of the Guardian, the Frankfurt group is "an unelected cabal made up of eight people (2016): Lagarde (IMF); Merkel; Sarkozy; Mario Draghi (president of ECB); Joée Manuel Barroso (president European Commission); Jean-Claude Juncker (chairman Eurogroup); Donald Tusk (president European Council) and Olli Rehn (Europe's Economic and Monetary Affairs commissioner). This group, which is accountable to no one, calls the shots in Europe".

Given the free reign which this cabal now exercises in its management of European, if not global financial matters, it's hardly surprising that money and power constitute the overriding theme of Eurozone ambitions. How many times have you heard, over the past few months, heads of state declaring that meetings must be concluded at such and such a time "in order to give the markets a clear message." Please note: not the people but the markets.

Everything, it now seems, is beholden to 'the markets'.

They have become a totem to which we are all expected to bow our heads in obeisance. The pervasive consumption and growth ideology and the covert lust for power which accompanies its pre-eminence suggest a deep sickness reaching into the heart of society. A sickness which gives licence to the establishment of technocratic dictatorships and the demotion of the instinct for democracy.

Jean Monnet no doubt recognised this at the inception of the European Union. Maybe he saw how a small group of well-schooled power-seekers would be able to engineer the economic collapse of Countries that failed to fulfil the diktats of the private club which he and his colleagues had instigated. Was it foreseen that it might be possible to achieve what the Reichstag had failed to achieve, but this time with little or no need for bloodshed?

In any event, gone is the Europe standing for a group of independent nation states banding together, when appropriate, on internationally significant issues. The entire edifice of the extended family of nations called Europe, has been brought to a point of crisis due to the artifice and brinkmanship of the executors of this global power grab. A power which now controls the media, the politicians, the market and the people. "We give them what we make them think they want" is an apt summary of the heist's blueprint for success.

In a world of mass media hype; virtual reality; 'shopping' as the number one leisure pursuit, plus every conceivable gizmo to play around with—one can see how the artful creation of these superficial distractions has combined to become such a powerful opiate.

Tragically, the bankrupt materialistic imagination of the modern European fails to penetrate the veil of deceit which has allowed the clandestine take-over to proceed so smoothly. As Aldous Huxley warned in Brave New World Revisited, 1958: "Democracy and Freedom will be the theme of every broadcast and editorial. Meanwhile the ruling oligarchy and its highly trained elite soldiers, police, thought-manufacturers and mind manipulators will quietly run the show as they see fit."

So here we stand, on the edge of the precipice, yet mostly failing to recognise that it is a precipice.

The federal superstate, currently managed by the infamous 'troika', is closing around us, regardless of any nation's membership or non-membership of the single currency regime. This control system works on the principle of keeping people just intelligent enough to serve the system but not intelligent enough to recognise that it is a system. It has been largely successful in this mission, since up until now we have been pacified into accepting the role of grudging servitude with few signs of outward resistance.

However, all that may be about to change. Signs of rebellion are appearing where once only the mists of sleep prevailed. The extremity of US and EU neo-colonial warmongering in The Middle East, Africa, the Persian Gulf and Central Asia, is raising eyebrows and not a few hairs on the nape of the neck. Oil companies are turning in the usual profits; banks are barely humbled by their carefree profligacy of 2008/9, and multi-millionaires are created every week in extravagant game shows and lottery draws. All this while government-instigated austerity packages are bearing down on citizens struggling to make a reasonable living and hold onto some modicum of social responsibility and decorum. Something has to give. And probably more than Greece, Ireland and Portugal.

Our long-running pretence at being anything other than the schizoid and hypocritical society that we are, is finally falling away. The bare bones of the truth can no longer be disguised behind placatory rhetoric and artful deception. As the realisation of what stands in front of us grows, we have a very real choice to make: stand on our own two feet and free ourselves from the encircling tentacles of the Monnet and Delors inspired supranational dictatorship—or slide further under its control—losing our ability to forge our destinies for generations to come. The choice has never been so stark.

It's down to each of us to reach into richer soils and ensure that something altogether better is brought to birth.

The criminal duplicity of the mainstream journalist

We are faced by a shocking fact these days: much of the profession of journalism, and I speak of mainstream media journalism, has descended into alarming levels of printed and broadcast disinformation. One can now virtually count on the fact that what is being said on any topic of political significance, will be a carefully scripted trotting out of government and corporate propaganda.

That is not journalism. That is what George Orwell called 'Newspeak'.

It is a dangerous game which these news hacks are playing. Too often, they are witnessing one event and describing it as quite another event. Let me amplify this by looking at the stories emanating out of the Middle East.

It must be obvious to most of us by now that Russia, via Putin, is being held responsible for pretty much everything which is no longer working well for Western-engineered neo-liberal/neo-conservative hegemonic globalism. In fact, the stream of accusations against Putin's Russia have descended into near or actual farce, due mainly to the fact that they are not backed by any factual evidence. We are all simply supposed to 'know' that Mr. Evil is at it again and that the West must ready itself to take action against his 'tyrannical activities'.

Aleppo: the BBC reported that returning pro-Assad Syrian army troops are raping and murdering the civilian population of this once beautiful city in Eastern Syria. That thousands were trying to flee the massacre going on night and day at the hands of Assad's army, supported by Russia and Iran. That a systematic bombardment of the citizens of West Aleppo was being perpetrated by the liberating Syrian army. That children were being killed in schools and that all this was being done with cold-blooded ruthlessness at the hands of the liberators.

You've seen this sort of 'journalism'. It is based on fictitious information concocted and spread about by paid-off insiders, hired to tell lies at ten a minute. They are there to protect the geopolitical interests of the West. As if to officially rubber-stamp this fact, the US Senate recently introduced a bill attempting to ban any story line which might contradict such 'official' version of events. Especially those surrounding the defeat of ISIS and the liberation of Aleppo which had been occupied—and virtually starved out—by ISIS terrorists for at least four years.

Attempts to silence truth are a direct attack on free speech. And such attacks are endemic in Westminster and Washington, as we have long been aware. But what we have been less focused on is the fact that mainstream media journalists are fully complicit. They are equally as worthy of the title 'criminals' as the editors who pay them to lie and the politicians who use these lies to further their ambitions.

I strongly doubt that any BBC, or other mainstream Western journalist, set foot in Aleppo during the time these reports were being issued. They didn't have to. The propaganda machine works best when nobody looks the reality in the eye. With some notable exceptions, they are simply puppets, singing the hymns that NATO, the EU and USA want the world to hear.

What happened in Aleppo is actually a disarmingly opposite reality. The Syrian national army had completed its recapture of the town. Supported by Russia and Iran, it has finally driven out the blood-curdling terrorist executioners who had held thousands of terrified Syrian citizens hostage and in fear of their lives. The liberating army brought food and reconnected drinking water supplies. It provided medical services to the sick and wounded and bussed others out of still active danger zones. It was greeted with relief and tears of joy. This I learned from a very reliable witness who was actually there.

While, in comparison with the West, Russia has emerged as a relative powerhouse of studied diplomacy, as well as an effective military force in directly combating the US and UK's gruesome hegemony.

ISIS, let us not fail to reveal, had even bombarded the people of Aleppo in their own homes, as a deliberate ploy so as to directly accuse Russia and Syria of engaging in these horrors. Western sponsored NGOs are also complicit in inverting such news horror stories to sound like the evil is being perpetrated by President Assad's national army. There is no end to the attempts being made to distort and reverse the reality.

Now, let's switch for a moment to that other closely related story of lies and deceit called 'Fake News'. And, lo and behold, the gods of what is brazenly called 'serious news' (the mainstream media empire) are suddenly spooked by the fact that they might be losing control over their people. That the feast of lies is not being absorbed as readily as before and that a significant number of those still able to think are turning over to alternative sources of information in search of something plausible.

Well, well, this is clearly something that must not be allowed to happen! Let's brand these clandestine truth-seeking sites 'Fake News' outlets, spreading false propaganda and lies amongst our audiences! Let's outlaw freedom of speech—err, I mean fake news—and impeach those who defy us. Yes, and now we 'know' Russia hacked into the US elections let's try and get the West on a serious war footing and kick NATO into action against these anti-Western infidels!

So what I have discovered concerning what actually occurred in Aleppo is now Fake News, and because I'm telling fake news I'm in danger of being criminalised and held up as a traitor of mainstream 'serious' news and no doubt my Country. Don't worry, I've been on the front lines for years fighting the likes of Monsanto, Tesco and the European Union, and I'm not about to run and hide at the behest of Rupert Murdoch, George Soros or the Rothschilds.

In a heightened state of outrage a few days ago, I contributed the following comment to a discussion on fake news in The Guardian: "You have just been reading a fake news column. Mainstream media = Fake News. It is under the unbending thumb of corporate control, and thus editors of papers, such as this one, are tools of a system that will only allow into print that which is expurgated and typically rid of any attempt to tell the truth, rather than the 'newspeak' acceptable to the status quo. End of story."

And somewhat to my surprise it was not moderated out of existence. It received support and dissent, but the support considerably outperformed the dissent.

Real investigative journalism can still be found in some mainstream press arenas; but it's under pressure all the time and therefore always in danger of being snuffed out altogether. Mostly, one has to look for information laid out on discerning alternative media sites in order to find out what's actually going on around the world. Please note that I said 'discerning'.

Mainstream journalists who knowingly distort the truth, especially in life and death situations, should be considered as directly complicit in crimes against humanity.

At the point of no return

The wrong people are in charge... that's pretty obvious. But what is not so obvious is how they got there. And once having found an open gate, why have we left them to graze the best pastures while we grovel around in the barren fallow? A very strange phenomenon...

This World is run by those of whom the great majority have absolutely no qualifications to be at the helm of anything – not even a small rowing boat. Yet, somehow or other, there they are perched in their palaces, surveying their empires, while simultaneously engaging in the systematic degradation of planet Earth.

Doesn't matter whether they are generals, headmasters, corporate executives, CEOs of banks, media moguls, ministers or prime ministers or just about any big bosses—they have the distinction of all acting in unison. While by contrast, the great majority of intelligent and able-bodied citizens of this planet, only manage to act—or react—in sporadic and discordant bursts; if at all.

The current controlling masters—and it hasn't changed much over many centuries—have a commonality of intent: to extract the last ounces of profit and prestige from any and all assets and opportunities that fall into their grasp.

Yet even that isn't enough for some of them. Profits get a bit boring when they come in the tens of millions year after year and one has occupied the prime suite at Claridge's for the past six months. No, there always needs to be just one more thing that can be 'owned' and brought under control, so as to satisfy the false aggrandisement that is part and parcel of an endless and ultimately fruitless attempt to become omnipotent and untouchable by ordinary mortals.

Such is the aphrodisiac called 'power'.

Time and again, those who suffer most from a sense of being inwardly dispossessed are the very ones to seek, as compensation, the maximum level of outer possessiveness. And this is the mechanism whereby the wrong people get to be in charge.

Ironically, many who do not suffer such delusional power urges, are quite happy to just tick along fulfilling their aspirations and daily needs as best as they can. Yet in doing so, they unwittingly allow the megalomaniacs a direct route to the seats of power.

Those who are secure enough in themselves to take a responsible attitude towards the life around them, seldom come forward to take on positions of authority and civic responsibility. Their preference is to leave it to others, and in too many cases these 'others' often harbor barely disguised ulterior motives.

Yet we look on, aghast, as our world is torn apart by duelling crooks and madmen, each more desperate than the other for the top job in the race for planetary ecocide. Each more desperate than the other to fill any power vacuum that might emerge. Each more desperate than the other to hold a cosh over the disinterested daily workers who struggle on, trying not to notice how bad it's become.

Where do you belong in this mad scrummage?

The wrong people are in charge and the right people don't want to take undue trouble to do anything about it. That just about sums up the dire state of our post-industrial 'civilisation'. Something has to give...

The question is what?

Will a critical mass of the 99% finally act to bring back some genuine self-autonomy through wresting control from the 1%?

Or will the 1% finally complete their annihilation job, trashing our planetary assets and crushing our human propensities once and for all? That is the question...

But none of us are free to sit back and play at second guessing the outcome. We are all in there. We are part of the pack. Our every move, whether we see it or not, is either promoting or resisting the despots' master plan. There is no such thing as being 'in between' in this game. The fence you once sat on is broken. The wires are hanging limp. There is no no-man's-land left to hide in.

At some point soon, those who are fit to lead must take over from those who are unfit. It may be a bloodless coup, or it may be a bloody insurrection. One way or another, the shift has to happen.

Forget about divine intervention. There will be no divine intervention unless and until there is a very visible human determination already out of the starting blocks and heading for the finishing line. Only then is it possible that higher energies will join the race to bring justice back to this battered World.

We are approaching the point of no return. If we don't respond to the myriad calls for help that are echoing around this World at an ever-increased velocity each day, then we will be condemning ourselves to being forever stranded upon a desolate and barren shore.

Any help starts with helping each other to break free from our learned and self-induced state of fear and pacifism. A combination that pretty much guarantees an unwillingness to act. An unwillingness to act even when presented with the choice of participating in a mass genocide or opposing it.

I use the word 'pacifism' here to convey a 'state of withdrawal' in face of the need to act. I do not refer to the choice, which everybody has, to refrain from violence. These are two very different conditions. In this context, taking the decision not to act with violence is an action. Taking no decision, but simply retreating into a shell, is not.

This unwillingness to act is giving voice to the notion that 'no action' is the spiritual choice of the knowing. That to retire into a cul-de-sac of meditation and inward looking self-examination can 'change the world' by dint of a shifted value focus. Can serve to hermetically seal the self away from the trials and tribulations of the outer world and thereby help avoid any confrontation with that which demands a full and spontaneous response.

Confrontation, in this view, is a negative, reactionary manifestation that undermines 'peace' and the supposed tranquility of a chimeric world which takes over from rational observations and becomes the new reality. A 'virtual reality'.

This is a deeply flawed and dangerous ethos. For it splits in half that which is whole and sets the two halves in opposition to each other.

We are 'of nature' not above or outside it. We go forth and we return. That is the Tao. Universal forces all dance to this tune. Breath, ocean waves, cycles of birth and death, growth and decay, all is in motion and at rest, all the time. There is no contradiction. Outward action and inward contemplation are two halves of one whole. They are synonymous. One should move between the two constantly and joyously.

"When injustice becomes law, resistance becomes duty"

Well, injustice has become law—yet resistance remains doggedly muted and the search for an escape route remains the preferred option.

Cultivate spirit, wisdom and deep awareness—yes. Yet not as an alternative to toppling our oppressors from their corporate thrones, but as part of it.

Don't be fooled. There is a war on. We are all called to the front. Just as the white corpuscles of our bodies are fighting off attempts by the pathogens to take hold, all the time. We should be doing the same, all the time.

Every day we should be conjuring up and putting into effect actions to end the draconian government/corporate dictatorship that continues to herd great swaths of humanity ever faster towards a sheer and genocidal cliff.

We can have no 'peace' until the criminals at the master control consulate are ejected from their padded leather chairs and are forced to confront the true price of their obscene power games.

Peace—and enlightenment, at the individual level, is only possible if we are engaged in this battle. The battle to rid both ourselves and this planet of that which seeks to dominate and destroy the true well-spring of life.

The road to victory also requires the wise and aware to form a council of responsible oversight to step into the void once the despots are dethroned. That is an essential ingredient of any uprising determined to manifest genuine justice.

The lessons of history teach that fickle rebellion simply replaces one bunch of power predators with another. That is no longer an option; we are now at the point of no return. This time we have to get it right.

Sold a lie

'The show must go on' as they say in the theatre. And indeed, so it would appear. Only this particular show seems to have no beginning or end. The curtain never comes down;

there isn't even an interval in which to draw breath and stretch one's legs.

It's a 24/7 bonanza, and the cost of a seat is almost certain to put you out of pocket. In spite of which, the auditorium is full of expectant faces staring up at the unfolding scenes and drinking in the drama being staged for their consumption.

So few actors, so many spectators. Yet the actors hold the attention and the spectators soon forget that they are in a theatre and have paid for their seats.

We are all at this performance. Its setting is planet Earth. The actors strut around feigning importance, playing the role ascribed to them by the writer of the script and the director of 'the show'. You know who they are – you see them every day on TV screens and newspapers. A few are quite convincing, and like most actors they feign true sincerity and then pause for the applause.

The director remains largely invisible, but in the background he has fixed the agenda and set the scene. The script writer also remains largely incognito. However, his words on the page provide the narrative without which the actors would not be able to perform their predesignated roles.

The cast of a recent crowd-pulling drama had names like May, Merkel and Trump. The play in which they performed had the title 'If I Ruled the World', and there are many other roles for aspiring lesser performers and even for some retired leading lights of yesteryear.

New scripts continuously emerge so as 'to keep the show on the road'. A recent hit, for example, was 'Brexit', a play in four acts, featuring a strong line-up of music hall performers as well as some fine orators, one of whom cut his teeth in the great performing venues of Continental Europe.

But look, these marionettes of the political charade called 'democracy' can only be where they are, and do what they do, because we give them centre stage. We let ourselves become embroiled in their show and convince ourselves that it's the only show in town. But it's not, and in spite of being big and noisy, it's actually a facade designed and orchestrated by the hidden hands who pull the strings that tweak the marionettes into action. Very occasionally a true leader emerges. An individual who stands out for their empathy with a struggling humanity.

However, for decades now, it is 'the show' that has contrived to dominate. A show kept in place by stage managers who ensure that all the rules, regulations and disciplines are operating as they should. But it is we the people who elect the cast of this play. A cast who promise to reflect and represent our needs on the national stage. To bring change where change is needed and to stand firm in the role that they are given.

So you see, we are complicit in the maintenance of 'the rules of the game' that keep the control system under which we suffer, alive and well.

Those whom we elect mostly fall at the first hurdle and all their promises go with them. 'The system' is in charge, after all, and our elected representatives quickly fall under the spell of its mechanics and become victims of its sinister agenda. An agenda played out on the global stage with the help of powerful centralised banks, mega corporations and a heavily funded military. Yes, this is the show we have paid to bring to town.

But we have been sold a lie. We have bought into a chimera, a charade, and the biggest part of the problem is that we fail to recognise this fact. We actually believe it is a bona fide happening, without which we would all be thrown into chaos and despair.

So it is that we cling on to this outworn model of 'democracy', fearful of what might happen if it were dismantled and consigned to history. Fearful maybe, of what might emerge in its place.

But that's no good, and you know it. Because what stands in front of us is a choice; to remain a slave to a system which cannot survive without slaves, or to break free and give form to something altogether different.

Are you ready to take such a step?

So what might bringing about something altogether different actually involve? We must have a go at answering this, because it is the most critical question of this era, one we all face today— whether we realise it or not.

What we are talking about is taking back control of our destinies, not giving responsibility for them to someone else. Try to conceive what this might be like... Well, for a start, out goes 'the politician' and with him/her the central control system called 'parliament'. By the way, parliament did once represent the venue for an ideal in the making. An aspiration to give voice to those who never had a voice and to introduce collective justice where only the will of a monarch had previously prevailed.

But such a situation has long been redundant, because parliament was hijacked decades ago by the hidden hand of centralised control, and the politician became a stooge for the banking, military and corporate power cartels seemingly beyond his control. That is why this 'corrupted beyond repair' model has to go.

There's a new lightness in the air at the sheer mention of such an action! What is mainstream media going to talk about without the mock democracy to fill its airwaves? Where will attention be turned once the charade of politics is removed from its pompous pedestal? What would we like to see fill the vacant place?

Think about it, because almost nobody is, and that is in large part the reason why it hasn't yet happened.

It is at around this point that something valuable starts stirring from the inside, and the seeds of a fresh vision put forth their first shoots. The low vibratory rate of energy to which we have adapted, shifts upward a gear. The fog starts to clear. We can see more clearly what we couldn't see at all before we dared dispense with the old lie.

The new perception looks and feels something like this: we are here on this world having something called 'a life'. It might last seven or eight decades, or more, or less; but as far as we know, it's the only one we've got (in this body). How did we acquire this special gift? What are we going to do with it? Since it's special and quite unique—isn't it logical that we would want to do something special and unique with it?

Once we see we've been sold a lie, our next logical realisation is to recognise that it's a massive waste of this one life we have, to pretend we can ignore reality. It is then that the possibility of something altogether different entering the arena, makes its unexpected debut.

"My God" it says "I want to live!" "I want to confront this lie head-on and cease running away from it!" And that is a truly revolutionary happening; one which can—in an instant—change our entire outlook on life. For although it's only a beginning, it's a real beginning, one full of promise for what might follow.

Looking back at the crazed and confused scenes taking place on the world stage, shifting like tides between high melodrama and low bestiality, we can now see that it is no use trying to paper over the cracks and pretend that we can go on living life 'as usual'. The cracks are the dominant factor and what lies in between is so insubstantial as to be of no practical use.

Our only way forward is to invent a new future. Open a fresh page in the book of life. Not ignoring the past, but getting to grips with understanding it, and then bringing it with us on the great new journey upon which we have embarked. Let a new-found passion lead the way. Let intuition be your guide. Let awareness be your tool box.

If you had identified yourself with any facet of the crumbling status quo, you will soon find yourself untethered, because there is nothing left able to hold a stake to which you can attach yourself.

There is nowhere left to turn except into your own inner resources. For it is from this region that the new vision emerges. That place where truth still resides, untrammelled by the ways of the world.

And then, on peering ever deeper within, one can begin to see the emerging presence of another world altogether. A world awaiting birth. Longing for birth. Waiting to be born. A world shimmering with expectation and excitement. A world lit up by luminous energies.

Men and women alike give birth to this great entity. It does not require a womb or a phallus, although its composition embraces the essence of female and male, finally liberated to give full focus to the building of the new society which it is our imperative to create.

Now is the time to set aside all that would try to close the window on our true destinies.

Here is where we will find the footings, the solid ground, from which we can start building the World to Come. A place to carry us through the storm which cannot be bypassed. That is our true work from now on.

The mad actors who strut the world stage today do not realise that they are playing out the final scene of an apocalyptic epic. A drama devised and directed by the architects of control. Criminals, whose full exposure is ever closer at hand.

We are moving into an auspicious time. A time in which mankind frees itself from the prison that has for so long held it hostage. An event which will break the cords of fear-induced captivity and finally bring down the curtain on this devious age of deception.

Reassessing Religion

A brief history of mind control from the christian cross to the mobile phone tower

For a long time now, some force alien to the spiritual and humanistic evolution of humanity has been working hard to subvert, and then reverse, the true awakening of human consciousness.

This force, working with both words and symbols, has effectively sidetracked humanity for its own ends. Erecting countless barriers on the path that leads to conscious awareness.

Quite a feat! Especially when one considers that, somewhere within, all of us are primed to react positively to love, joy, creativity and exploration of the unknown.

Any force or entity intending to squash that lot must surely have access to some pretty advanced insights. Insights into just where to find the potential fissures in our 'state of wholeness'. And then, to know exactly what to do to ensure that they are prized open and made extremely difficult to close again!

We recognise how subliminal advertising has the power to direct the subconscious element of the human brain to react in ways that are advantageous to those doing the advertising; but typically disadvantageous to those impulsively caught by the irrational desire to buy whatever it is that is being advertised.

Imagery, especially that dressed with an emotional content, has the power to become transfixed in the neocortex. Producing a stream of irrational thoughts that, if allowed to prevail, lead the individual into a prison of his or her own making.

One of the most ubiquitous and effective of these emotionally charged images is the Christian cross. It was to become a symbol with an almost unique power to imprison its adherents.

On its own, this cross already achieves a certain degree of penetration of the subconscious and indeed conscious mind; but with the addition of the forlorn figure of Jesus nailed and roped onto its crossbar, it instantly triples in power.

Why is this?

Of course, we know the answer: an entire galaxy of emotionally charged feelings, views, opinions and uncertainties are instantly drawn, like moths to a flame, around this image; thanks to our mass indoctrinations into the Western religious belief system called Christianity.

We can see that to be an effective indoctrination mind-controller, one first needs to establish a powerful symbol/image and then imbue it with a meaning which will serve the end one desires to bring about.

Two thousand years after the crucifixion, the image in question still arouses in followers of the Christian doctrine—and even many non-followers—a kind of diluted, tepid form of compassion. Also the emotion of 'shame'; the emotion of 'guilt'; the emotion of 'mystic adoration'. Emotions which add-up to a pervasive sense of sadness. A subconscious inner submission. Submission to the doctrinaire persuasions of the Christian tradition. The ones which teach that, since our 'fall' in the Garden of Eden, we are all 'sinners' and therefore in some way responsible for the demise of a great saint.

Now just consider the extraordinary power of repression which is built into accepting a criminal involvement in the death of one who is claimed to be the Son of God! Consider the power carried by the highly charged image of the cross upon which this martyr was crucified. An image whose age-old tenure can be explained by its emanating just the right mix of genuine and false emotional signals. Simultaneously and cruelly playing upon valid human emotions as well as the utterly falsified convictions which form the dogma of 'religious obeisance to the fallen martyr'.

What a subtle and potent trap!

Now images and symbols can—and do—also work for the common good. For the inspiration of mankind. When devised by the hand of the 'artist of good intent', symbols stir the corpuscles of our higher consciousness, putting us in touch with our deeper selves. All great artists have created and continue to create such imagery.

Even the cross, in its more pagan form, as in the Celtic cross, exudes a positive resonance, seeming to centre the viewer in a spiritually harmonious way. This is not mind control, but mind liberation.

Whereas the Christian cross, by dint of the lateral bar being three quarters of the way up the execution pole, places the emphasis of the image elsewhere. The crucifixion of criminals on these stakes was, I learned recently, a common occurrence at the time of Jesus. The high position of the cross bar emphasises the upper body and head at the expense of the lower body. In this, it encourages the formation of a split, where in fact there is no split. Mind body and spirit are 'whole', which the more pagan Celtic cross appears to recognise.

But the introduction of an upward aspiring theme plays neatly into the notion of salvation. And salvation is a critically important and indeed central concept of Christianity. One which has proved to be the downfall for millions upon millions of 'God-fearing' citizens of this planet, for at least the last two millennia.

Why link salvation to a 'downfall'?

Because it has played straight into the hands of the architects of top-down control. It has left man feeling— and therefore being— impotent and powerless; always hoping and expecting to be saved from his (mostly non-existent) sins, by a distant and all-powerful patriarch. A patriarch who might or might not, offer forgiveness; depending upon just how often and how earnestly the one on his knees maintains his/her cry for 'forgiveness'.

It is here that we find the source, or at least one of the most significant sources, of the blanket passivity displayed by those who should have been exhibiting the opposite tendency. Who should have been actively involved at the very helm of positive change, right from the beginning.

With millions indoctrinated to believe that 'there is nothing to be done other than pray for God to intervene', our planet became an open book for hard line interventionists, Masonic cults, Illuminati control agents and various other secret society manipulators. We can see just how easily those willing and able to exploit human weakness, have capitalised on a salvation-susceptible humanity; giving rise to thousands of years of almost continuous manipulation of the prevalent servile mentality. A mentality brought about by seeing one's self as a largely powerless entity, and that which one worships as being the voice of absolute authority.

For people in the thrall of this unseen 'patriarchal god', all society authority figures simply become subliminal reproductions. Reproductions of the 'first' dominant patriarch. Even those who have been elected to office by their followers are then allowed to dominate and introduce regulations that rarely are in the interest of the people.

Followers of 'the faith', probably without realising it, thus become the servants of their self-created idols. Never mind if they are dressed in cassocks, pin striped suits or sports kits.

What was set in motion from the outset by the architects of control, was a widespread tendency in homo sapiens to offer unholy obeisance to anybody (or group of bodies) who seem to possess the aura of power and authority. This is what the Christian Church has, wittingly or unwittingly, been promoting since its inception; but with the tacit support and outright cunning of the masters of deception.

From here, there is just one step on to a long stream of capitulations by 'the people' to central control systems. Usually taking the form of exploitive 'democratic' governments, oligarchs, hegemonic corporations, the banking industry, the media corporation, the military-industrial war machine, Nazi-inspired trading blocs, all contributing to the eventual demise of planet Earth.

All of this could and should have been avoided. None of it needed to have happened. But the cunning powers of dark side subversion that played relentlessly on the inferiority complexes of indoctrinated Christian neophytes, plus the tens of millions of secular souls swept along by the dominant current of the age, were more successful than forces representing the passionate power and intent to respond to the call of consciousness.

Having successfully built a hierarchical pyramid-like control system into the very structure of everyday society, and found it essentially unchallenged, further phases of control followed one upon the other. And as the years of the twentieth century rolled into view, George Orwell, Aldous Huxley and other perceptive writers drew attention to further unfolding developments in the art of mind control. Those that would particularly be targeted on an (intentionally) war-torn Western Europe and a North American continent (intentionally) wallowing in a materialistic dream... Yet still the 'civilised world' of the religious faithful soldiered blindly on: "Onward, Christian soldiers, marching as to war, with the cross of Jesus going on before" as declares the refrain of a popular Christian Hymn. That cross just won't go away.

But the old forms of religious indoctrination did eventually start to lose some of their pulling power. And this provided Orwell's Big Brother the cue to turn his attention towards a new kind of mass hypnosis.

A hypnosis designed to further strengthen the momentum of the Illuminati directed New World Order programme. To get it to the point where 'full spectrum dominance' could be applied without anybody really noticing. Without it ever appearing as though it was being enforced. Without ever seeming to be anything other than voluntary acceptance by a public ever eager to savour the fruits of the 'convenience' life style which was being laid at their doorstep.

So it is that a new form of Christian cross became erected across the fields and dales of countryside expanses and on the roofs of town houses, schools and businesses. It was christened 'the mobile-phone tower'. Many paid obeisance to it.

The signals it transmitted were designed to do something very clever: to integrate themselves into the natural wave signals received by the human brain at 7.83 Hz, the same background vibrational pulse-pattern as that of the planet and its outer atmosphere—known as the Schumann Resonance. A natural balancing agent of human well-being.

Now there was no need for a 'cross' and an enforced message about its reverential qualities. There was a more direct route to the neocortex; one which could be used wherever and whenever it was deemed useful, to solicit information about the location and behaviour of just about anybody and everybody. To listen to conversations and to create, if deemed necessary, a further blockage of the development of human consciousness.

This microwave-emitting Tower of Babel was to readily find its place alongside pesticide-ridden and GMO denatured foods, polluted water supplies, engineered atmospheric disturbances and controlled weather. As well as dumbing-down TV transmissions; 24/7 high-tech surveillance apparatus and the wholesale propaganda exercise known as 'education' including its close cousin 'democratic government'.

Thanks to the mobile phone tower supplanting the Christian cross we can now Tweet and Twitter our way to the promised land of an ever more automated existence. One where the difference between a human and a machine become practically indiscernible. A blending which fulfils the coldly calculating goal of the Transhumanist agenda.

Lost in the wonderment of a WiFi world that increasingly 'does our thinking for us', we find the aptly named 'Cloud technologies'. Technologies that create an invisible, interlinked virtual microwave reality, sealing us off from the real world like a curtain pulled across a garden window.

While all the while, brains are slowly fried via the handsets that receive the microwave tower signals. Precious brains, that just might have shown us a whole other way of reaching the actual Promised Land. That place which, from the beginning, was our very special prerogative to create. A prerogative based upon our inherited powers of Godliness. Powers stolen via the deliberate separation of man from God, as exemplified by the infamous sacrificial cross.

Now, with our world on the brink, we have no choice other than to find the courage to bring forth in ourselves that which is our true power. A power which has refused to die, in spite of all. Our divine gift. The only power that can still, even at this late stage, overcome the sycophantic architects of control and finally bring to birth the glorious reality we came here to make manifest. There's no point in contemplating failure. That process points straight back to the execution pole. Those who carelessly allow their finest spirit to wither away, should ask themselves this question: Just what is it that is being sacrificed?

Original sin—a myth whose time is up

Of all the deceptions pulled on humanity over the ages, Original Sin is probably the most devastating. Yet hugely successful from the perspective of the perpetrators.

Almost everywhere the doctrine of Christianity forged its zealous mission to convert the masses, so Original Sin accompanied it. Imposing the rationale of guilt on untold millions whose open minds no doubt thought they were receiving a message of emancipation and light.

Not so my friends, you were in fact receiving a message just about as dark as darkness gets!

The extraordinary power of a message, properly formed, packaged and publicised, is something we have all come to learn a lot about in recent decades. 'The medium is the message' declared Marshall McLuhan back in 1964. And that edict could easily pass for the moment the first biblical texts let it be known that a man called Adam and a woman called Eve got the whole human race off to a very bad start, from which it appears to have never recovered.

However, the reason it got off to a bad start and has still failed to fully recover, cannot be pinned on any fault of Adam and Eve, as we shall see, but lies squarely at the feet of a masterful plot to falsify what is actually a potent story of human emancipation and growing inner conviction.

This 'human race' to which the biblical text refers, was set on its way by a starting pistol fired by someone who didn't want anyone participating in this race to actually win. He or she or it only wanted losers; and that's pretty much what they got.

See what I mean by successful?

The story goes like this: there were just two human beings on this planet at the moment the starting pistol was fired. There was a beautiful garden as well, and in that beautiful garden were these two humans: a man called Adam and woman called Eve, and there was also an apple tree (in full fruit) and a serpent.

In this ensuing myth, God makes it clear to Adam that he can do whatever he likes in this garden except "eat of the fruit of the Tree of Knowledge." But, well, being human, and having been given 'free will' by divine rite, he doesn't really see the logic in this command from above. The serpent seems in accord with him in this, and somehow or other tempts Eve into plucking this big juicy apple and taking a bite before then offering it to Adam.

"And he did eat thereof. And the eyes of them both were opened, and they knew that they were naked; and they sewed fig leaves together, and made themselves aprons." They were, we are informed "ashamed." Both on account of taking a forbidden action and of being revealed unto themselves as "naked".

It is around this infamous 'eating of the fruit'—an action most of us would likely have taken out of simple curiosity—that millennia of Christian shame and guilt have their inception.

Here is where a pervasive irrational suffering concerning our natural physical condition has its origins. Where our 'private parts' became privatised. Where the natural pleasures of physical intimacy were turned to guilt: unless of course the so-called 'Church of God' authorised such acts via formal marriage in the Christian place of worship.

A great plethora of 'thou shalt nots' were soon pinned onto what was essentially Adam and Eve's courageous original act of 'civil disobedience': the refusal to be cowed by a seemingly higher authority.

Yes, by looking deeper into this infamous story, we see that Adam and his accomplice Eve did something pretty special in this Garden of Eden. Their action, when viewed in a manner freed from the typical conditioned response, looks very much like a 'giant step forward for mankind'. Something which Neil Armstrong was told to say once he put a foot on the moon.

Mythical Adam and his mythical Eve conspired to start a great ball rolling down the ages which would, one day, lead to man acquiring real knowledge, real independence and real self-awareness. Except, of course, that this was the last thing that the manipulators of this story wanted.

On further examining the symbolism of this tale, one can recognise that eating the apple of the Tree of Knowledge opened the eyes of this man and woman to the fact that they were adequately equipped to take their destinies into their own hands and forge their own path in life.

A path which would reveal to them that they were not just subjects to be ordered around according to the will of their master, but were blessed with a unique gift: the ability to think and act creatively and rationally. Even to reflect on their own condition and existence. And, equally contrary to the classic interpretation, it was indeed their Creator himself who wished this to be so.

For this Creator felt the pain of loneliness, and longed to have company in the great quest of life. But in order to have this company, his Adam and Eve had to pass the first great test: that of defying false authority and daring to eat from the Tree of Knowledge. Only then could they start on the road of becoming 'strivers with God' and companions to the supreme; blazing that uncharted course whose direction only becomes known through embracing the insecurity of the creative process. Taking that momentous 'leap in the dark' which is the mother of all great quests. All great adventures.

However, the biblical text upon which we were all raised, tells us something very different. It tells us that Adam and Eve were 'cast out' of this Garden of Eden due to their unforgivable and sinful act of disobedience. Disobedience to God himself, no less. Which caused them to be 'ashamed': both of their nakedness and their disobedience.

We are told by the church, which sees itself as the spokesperson of this biblical story, that thanks to Adam and Eve, we all carry 'the shame' to this very day. That we must pay the price of this 'original sin' and be humbled by the magnitude of this human error. An error of such supposed gravity that it became known as 'The Fall'.

In this translation of the stories surrounding certain key events of prehistory, man 'falls' before he has even begun to walk—and everything that follows is tainted by this supposedly tragic error of human judgment.

What does this Nakedness really symbolise?

It is the moment when we realise that everything we thought was one thing actually turns out to be another. A lot of stuff drops off us in that instant. We become naked, because the old clothes don't fit any more and the new clothes have to be woven from fresh wool. It is the dawn of true knowledge. Knowledge that makes us aware that there exists a divine state—and also a corruption of that state. That, at any one time, both exist. And that we must choose our course in life based on this knowledge.

The Garden of Eden is representative of a state of essentially 'passive' potential. An as yet unignited and unmoving potential. What was needed was a spark to set the whole thing off. And that spark came when Eve, who was in subconscious communication with the serpent, reached up and plucked that ruddy round apple and took a bite out of it. It was she who broke the 'obeisance to authority' taboo.

How about The Serpent's role in this drama?

The serpent is the anima of a rising energy. The Kundalini serpent, entwined around the spine (trunk) of the tree of knowledge.

When the serpent spoke to Eve, it was 'The Word'. "In the beginning was The Word". However, this word was not an actual word, but a vibration. An impulse. Energy directed from within. And this energy said to Eve "Do It". And she did. Her action bears the hallmark of the first stirrings of a divine mission: the stirring into movement of that which is fecund, yet unable to act.

The female divine force it was which enabled Adam and Eve to 'come awake' and find that they were no longer just innocent hippies frolicking in the cosy garden of the unconscious; unchallenged and unaware of the greater reality of existence. It is a prerogative of 'attaining the knowledge of good and evil' to then set off on that path of greater knowledge, no matter what! And what about The Tree?

The tree itself is a powerful symbol of growth. For it outwardly expresses the manifestation of a condition essential for man's own evolution: the putting down of roots and the spreading out and up of trunk and branches—as a simultaneous act. An act transmutable to us humans, almost literally; starting at the navel, where the umbilical cord has nourished us is the womb, and moving simultaneously down and up from here.

It has the great quality of annulling the 'either-or' option, which is the hallmark of much of our formal education. Real human development, in body mind and spirit, is both a tap root into the deep and a crown reaching into the beyond. In equal measure. Always both—never just one or the other.

So the Tree of Knowledge in the Garden of Eden is indeed just that: a tree of knowledge. It is not "the forbidden tree" as is commonly taught in the Christian church.

So why did the church choose to promote this forbidden factor?

Because this 'knowledge' is capable of exposing the tyranny that lies at heart of human slavery. A knowledge that must not be allowed out for fear of its repercussions on the control system which was already in place, and to which the church was—and remains to this day—an accomplice. The command 'not to eat' of the fruit of the Tree of Knowledge did not come from God, but from some other force implacably set against all that is divine.

As the story tells us: "around its trunk a serpent is entwined". From ancient times this serpent has been recognised as a source of special energy. Particularly, as said earlier, in the descriptions of the Kundalini practice of Tantra Yoga. It is the rising energy which illuminates, one by one, the seven chakras of the human body by moving up the spinal column; just as the serpent is moving up the trunk of the Tree of Knowledge, awakening (in this case) the succulent glory of the famous apple. A bite out of which moved Adam and Eve into a certain 'state of awareness'!

The serpent and the tree are thus powerful symbols—and tools of human enlightenment. And The Garden?

I have already alluded to the notion that the garden is a   place— or a condition—which remains untainted. In this it is a symbol of our childhood. A time when we were not yet conscious of historical karma and therefore able to freely explore all that which becomes manifest, within and without.

It's a place in which one remains, as in the case of the plant and animal kingdoms, in a state of instinctive response to divine energies, with as yet little or no involvement of individual will.

But that is not man's and woman's lot in life. Nor is it why our creator made manifest a state of 'conscious awareness', a state associated with the use of the higher mind.

In order to activate this higher mind Adam and Eve could not remain forever in their childhood garden, but needed to 'eat from the tree of knowledge' thus recognising the actual challenge that lay ahead. The challenge of moving from unconscious sub-awareness to conscious full awareness. From childhood to adulthood. A long and winding road indeed! But a road in which each step carries with it a fuller understanding of our greater role in the divine plan.

This is the 'road of genius' that British 18th century poet William Blake referred to when he wrote: "The straight road is a road of progress, but the crooked road is the road of genius." And the Divine Plan itself?

Ah, we are not really privy to the full architecture of the divine plan. For it is a 'state of being' and as such cannot really be described, only attained, through the lasting application of true intent.

However, I believe we can recognise that, put very simply, our Creator remembered his own coming into movement from that which lacked movement; and he wished to celebrate this, 'his birthday'. The day movement was born.

But one cannot celebrate a birthday without the presence of other empathising beings with whom to share the joyous occasion. So 'in the beginning' this creator was most fortunate in being visited by a complementary, yet opposite and deeply receptive energy.

This great coming together of opposite yet deeply complementary energies was of huge significance, because out of it emerged a state which we call 'equilibrium', movement. Something which is going somewhere, with a sense of purpose. No longer just a becalmed state of fecundity.

Movement owes its origins to a female energy. In Indian mythology this feminine force is called Shakti, the female principle of God. God, whose omnipotence expresses the consummated marriage of the creative and receptive principles, is thus dual in nature. Both male and female; female and male. And everything in this universe is an expression of this duality. Everything that comes to life, comes to life through the friction made manifest by this hugely potent and divine love affair. A love affair between the two energetic components of a primordial and primal duality. The ever-present Yin and Yang of existence.

And what we call sexuality is actuality 'sex-duality', the consummated act of divine union which gave birth and made manifest what we call Life. And perhaps most wonderful and mysterious of all is that an omnipresent and omnipotent force called Love infused and nourished this great primordial act of union which we ourselves are an expression of. One might even say that this Love preceded the one we call the Creator ... but that is another story in our deep and unfathomable past!

For now, it is enough to recognise that Adam and Eve, the Garden, the Tree and the Serpent, were all critical elements in kick-starting the evolution of mankind, and indeed all sentient life forms. We can now most clearly state that 'Original Sin' was precisely the opposite of a sin; it was the birth of man as a free agent in pursuing the divine intuitive message which leads us (back) to our Creator. But this time as responsible realised beings. As microcosmic Gods in our own right.

Then the Creator will greatly rejoice at the results of this divine union and will welcome us to the Great Celebration which cannot happen until the moment of our participation, as equals, in his Godliness. An event keenly anticipated by sowers of truth—and greatly feared by spreaders of the lie.

All the confusions surrounding sexuality and sexual relations stem from this distortion called Original Sin. Our sexuality, far from being something to be ashamed of, is that which connects us directly with the Divine. It was, I repeat once again, due to that glorious consummation between two poles of irresistible mutual attraction—male and female—that this Universe came to life. That 'life' which forms the birthplace of our very own cosmic essence.

Only something expressing an extreme position of alienation to this joyous truth would wish to lay such a sinister and divisive trap for mankind. A trap which, by proclaiming the celebration of our sexuality 'a sin', epitomises the state of reversed truth which still remains central to the workings of our strangled Western societies.

What that force is which is so adept at twisting truth into its opposite is another story for another time.

For now, let us take pleasure in having put the divine plan right back on track. On having reconnected to the roots of our true nature and found that, far from being ashamed we are proud to go forward in full knowledge of our innate divinity.

Let us rejoice in the fact that this innocuous debacle known as Original Sin has been properly exposed as a deeply divisive myth whose time is well and truly up. May it finally crumble to dust under the iridescent rays of a rising Aquarian sun!

Waiting for God

After the recent carnage in France, the Dalai Lama was asked what should be done concerning such atrocities on this planet, and if he thought people should pray for Paris? This statement formed the central part of his answer:

"We cannot solve this problem only through prayers. I am a Buddhist and I believe in praying. But humans have created this problem, and now we are asking God to solve it. It is illogical. God would say, solve it yourselves because you created it in the first place."

So fundamental is the truth behind this response that it should serve to eradicate any doubts left lingering in the minds of those who believe that only divine intervention can save them—or indeed the planet—from whatever it is that threatens to overwhelm both.

I am not a Buddhist, but if that is a central tenet of the Buddhist philosophy, then all power to the practitioners! The Dalai Lama's proclamation is rooted in deep common sense, and deep common sense surpasses religious belief and faith. It is a missing link in this world of virtual reality smoke and mirrors, in which far too many seem to feel that anybody 'but they' should take responsibility for helping to reset the life direction of this beleaguered planet.

In a vague sort of way many individuals appear to be waiting for someone, or thing, to make the decisions they don't want to make. To take the steps they don't want to take. To intervene and make things OK.

For others, the unwillingness to take responsibility often equates with the belief that life is essentially composed of random and chaotic events that have little or no meaning and no connection with each other. For these members of the human race, taking responsibility involves some sort of attempt to create an order. Strictly man made. Not a reflection of any all-pervading cosmic order. Definitely not 'as above—so below'. More likely 'as below' full stop!

Of these two lineages, the most deceitful is the first. The one which continuously shifts responsibility onto a third party and then seeks refuge in a higher power. Seeks solace in the fact that 'another' will surely sort out the problems one has brought upon one's self or the planet, by refusing to take a stand. This attitude constitutes a singular failing within much of humankind. Mainly, as the Dalai Lama so clearly states, due to the sheer illogicality of adopting such a position in the first place.

Yet disowning the need to participate in making change is widespread; as is the "there is no higher power/God" position. Between them, they probably account for the majority living in Western style democracies and maybe a similar percentage in other regimes.

So where does this refusal to accept 'response-ability' have its inception? This unwillingness to acknowledge and act on one's innate ability to respond to that which clearly demands a response? For thousands of years the planet has been in the grip of top-down controlling regimes, many of which have been quite ruthless in maintaining their authority. Even with the advent of 'democracies', elitist, top-down political structures remain the norm. The only exception to the power-seeking self-interests common to both, are benign dictatorships in which wise and compassionate individuals have supported the wider socio-economic and cultural interests of their nations. There is another one: the tribal peoples of the world who acknowledge the wisdom of the tribal elders and maintain a close association with the natural environment. A position which is also common to almost all genuinely agrarian communities.

For the rest, however, life has been mostly about surviving under an insidious and persistent form of top-down repression, essentially lasting for millennia.

Of course, those who, by one means or another, managed to develop and maintain links with the ruling classes, life was probably quite bearable or even good. But they learned that one has to play one's cards astutely; and then to accept the consequences, which involved living a kind of pretend existence in which obeisance to the master can never be dropped.

With the rise of organised religion, the downtrodden people found solace in the idea that a benign god could lighten their load, and that obeisance to this heavenly master offered some escape—at least for the mind—from the impositions of their earthly masters. The church let it be known that only this god could bring the greater change so many desired. Thus under this regime, people were once again absolved from the need to make the change happen themselves.

Where within this picture I have painted, is there any opening for the rise of an enlightened faction willing and able to take responsibility for helping set a new direction for life on this planet? It seems to me that the odds were stacked against the sort of liberation of spirit that could achieve this form of breakthrough. Where it was perhaps possible, for instance during the European Renaissance period, it was the artists who had gained favor with the aristocrats that led to the explosion of light, color and form symptomatic of that period. But little or nothing was done to help spark a revolution for the emancipation of the people. Many artists, those who were best placed to stir the sparks of a greater action, retreated into ivory towers, concentrating their concerns on their own creative endeavors. Does that sound familiar?

Thus it seems likely to be the case that we have no genuine precedent for what is now called for. The reason why so few 'take responsibility', beyond fulfilling the functions of daily life, is because for millennia it simply wasn't something 'people did'.

It was the job of the masters, both secular and religious, to set the agenda and for everyone else to follow. The church introduced its own form of hierarchy and berated the people for their non-conformist sins. Cajoling millions into believing that the authority of a highly judgemental 'God' must be respected if they wanted to avoid going in the wrong direction after death.

The church thus misinterpreted the teachings of Jesus Christ and declared that 'The Divine' is separate from the human and that one's duty is to pray and to remain passive, even in times of crisis.

Millions of congregations around the planet have been encouraged to believe that the Messiah will return and offer salvation to all those of a pious nature and humble mind. And that, in the meantime, there is nothing much they could or should do other than pray for forgiveness and remain God- and Government-fearing citizens.

That largely remains the case today, even if the sources of influence have changed somewhat. So we should not be surprised to find that it's only the few who stand up to face the various crises besetting this planet. It is still only the few who seem able to take genuine response-ability and to manifest intention and action.

'Waiting for God' is not how most would describe their affliction of passivity and disinterest in challenging the status quo. Yet, the symptoms of this sickness are pretty much identical with those of former years.

The waking-up of the human race is contingent upon recognising the truth that humans have created this problem, and are now asking God to solve it. It is illogical. According to Dalai Lama, God would say "solve it yourselves because you created it in the first place."

God would surely be correct! There is no other way forward. But once we do take this step, the greater universal powers spring to our aid, revealing that after all we do possess divine powers and do not need to get permission from some authority to use them.

But in the meantime, the universal higher powers feel obliged to fill the vacuum left by a distracted and dumbed-down humanity. To save the planet from absolute destruction by wilful acts of psychotic madness that are almost a daily occurrence at this time.

Isn't it time to give them a break?

When the New Year dawns, make a pledge that it will be the time of giving back. The year of offering replenishment and nourishment to the Source which has unstintingly provided for us millennia after millennia. Time to show that we have it in us to enhance rather than destroy the gift of life that we have inherited. Time to take our Creator by the hand and proudly reveal the emergent powers of all that is innately divine and determined about us humans. Let us honor His ecstatic vision of the glorious and turn it into reality! The time of waiting for God to act is long passed, lost in the mists of time. The moment of rising to our own godliness is upon us. No more fruitless longing. The Messiah is Here and Now. We are his progeny, reborn as glowing lights in the midst of darkness and war. Casting aside the swaddling clothes of old. Rise up, emergent co-creators in a perfect storm of healing creativity.

Organic hierarchy or dark side deception?

According to the wisdom 'as above—so below' we can ascertain that a common principle and order apply to both the workings of this planet and to the cosmos. If so, we can surmise that, in their innocent forms, both work to a common and essentially hierarchical principle.

Do we accept the existence of such an order? Or is it so tainted here on Earth that the very word 'hierarchy' automatically raises the hackles of controversy?

I would suggest that it is not a question of ostracising hierarchy per se, but of exploring whether a 'natural hierarchical principle' emerges on Earth, as an organic expression of 'as above—so below.'

From the earthly perspective, gaining a foothold on the cosmic ladder requires a degree of conscious awareness. This becomes a more decisive factor when determining the qualities that are required to attain, for example, the status of 'a true teacher'.

That same status might also indicate having the wisdom and ability to govern. If so, we are starting to recognise what might be the critical foundation stones of a society which could ultimately replace the quasi-democratic mess we live in today.

There is no doubt many levels that make up the moving stairway to full conscious awareness; thus many roles to fill on the journey of aspiration towards the Supreme. A society which embraces this form of aspirational governance will offer countless rungs of 'employment' for its people, each reflecting and drawing out the actual talents and creative abilities each individual possesses.

Here we move far beyond the modern day pseudo-democratic experiment in which individual aspiration is honored to the degree that it devotes itself to the acquisition of wealth, prestige and a well-honed ability 'to play the game'. A game which the status quo has set up in order to maintain its entirely false hierarchical ambitions.

Nevertheless, the idea of establishing a hierarchy here on Earth is likely to have its origins in an attempt to mirror the universal model. That is why the wisdom of the phrase 'as above—so below' carries such a particular significance.

'As above—so below.' What does it mean to you?

We are mostly trapped in our understanding of what an 'order of merit' actually is. This is because we have been educated to believe that 'an order of merit' means 'an order of importance'.

An order that attributes prestige and power in ever larger doses according to the importance of the role being occupied.

Thus, in this distortion of the cosmic order, some are important while others are less important and others are not important at all. From kings and queens all the way 'down' to plebs and peasants.

Yet draw back and view this pyramid from a distance and you will see that every layer of it is equally significant; for every layer supports every other layer. Remove the plebs and the peasants, and the base of the pyramid collapses, bringing down the kings and queens with it!

So, in fact, we can conclude that the peasants and plebs are actually the most 'important' to the integrity of this structure, and not the least, as the status quo likes to maintain.

Now let's look at the 'as above' version of this story.

Here we find a similar basic design, but one which attaches no greater importance or prestige to any level within the structure, which runs from Supreme Consciousness to archangels, angels and on to devas and spirits. I use these names more descriptively than insisting on their reality.

In the 'as above' version, the levels of leadership—for want of a better word—are fully expressed in each stratum of the planes of consciousness: fourth, fifth, sixth, seventh and beyond. And the result is a virtual (or actual) ladder which every existing level of consciousness can use to get to the next one, or even to return to an earlier one. As in the Bodhisattva tradition of a return to Earth to help others get beyond the static confines of a uniquely third density state.

There are likely 'commanders-in-chief' operating at the universal level as well as on the earthly plane. The formal structure of our military is maybe just an imitation of universal high command's hierarchies and various levels of active implementation.

'As above—so below' seems to be inviting us to recognise and implement the cosmic design here on Earth. Because, in regards to the functioning of the life principle—as opposed to the human distortion of it—all of nature is in a constant state of mirror-like response to differing frequencies of universal energies, and is offering up its own unique reflection of these energies in return.

It is a symbiotic relationship of which all parts are in essence 'divine', and none more important than the other. They are all expressions of a Supreme Consciousness. This is the 'holistic' or 'quantum' state of understanding which certain elements of humanity are grappling with at this time; and all elements would be grappling with if our society operated in harmony with the cosmic truth 'as above—so below'.

However, where human evolution should be based upon 'highest wisdom' and 'divine teachers', the distorted version has instead created 'hierarchical elites' and 'autocratic authority figures'.

This is not necessarily a purely Earth oriented deviation. It is more than possible that it has its origins in early cosmic history. However, wherever it began, the distortion has spread ubiquitously, and is currently testing the veracity of the divine order at all levels.

We see that the Earthly 'status quo deviants' have deliberately used the divine model hierarchy, as described earlier—and cunningly distorted it, so as to make it appear to operate according to an impregnable order here on Earth. One which also takes direction from a 'supreme authority' figurehead—or number of such posers.

This is the parasitic genius of what are known variously as Archons, Gyns, Flyers or, in the West, Demons. They are parasitic, non-human deceivers that twist the truth into its opposite. They have successfully spun their slippery 'matrix' web of deceit, distortion and death here on Earth, where there should instead be manifest honesty, truth and life, headed by a council of wise and spiritually mature statesmen.

The Archons work through human beings. And here on earth, those possessed by their parasitic energetic forces are usually those who claim ancestry to god-kings of ancient Babylon, reptilian overlords and ultimately to Lucifer, the supreme epitome of poisoned darkness and undisputed king of the underworld.

The roles of the divine dimensional energies are here usurped by the dark side's determination to invert the true cosmic order for its distorted own ends.

In doing so, 'as above—so below' is proclaimed in its opposite order 'as below-so above'; thus making sure that 'as below' is indeed the place where man's power resides. The power of total possessive control, as opposed to a divine order which teaches complete non attachment.

'As above' then becomes a projected universal extension of the 'as below' format. The 'insentient man as god' syndrome.

I believe that we are therefore mistaken should we rule that hierarchy is in itself a purely exploitive concept. It is simply that the cosmic ladder to the Supreme, which is composed of different levels of consciousness each offering the other a leg-up, if you like, has been deliberately reversed into a fascistic, self-serving, elitist power pyramid.

The hierarchical order whose omega point is the Supreme, is an organic hierarchy; which if reflected on Earth, would surely guide us to the Promised Land.

Therefore, in order to fully understand why the Illuminati master plan is so effective, we must first recognise that it is modelled upon the divine master plan, aping the divine evolutionary blueprint. And in doing this, it provides an almost perfect false alibi to the population of the planet.

Religion plays its part in furthering this 'divine illusion' since it too boasts a structure that demands obeisance to a false hierarchical order and priesthood.

In both cases this 'order' is a fake version of the true order. It is an entirely static construction which has been built to keep power strictly within the domain of the perpetrators of deception.

Heaven on Earth, in the terms of the Illuminati matrix, is when banking kings, pharmaceutical giants, oil and agribusiness conglomerates and military hardware exponents—have finally stitched up the global control agenda—and produced their 'new world order' of compassionless automatons, maintained in their comfort zones by those dehumanised, servile citizens who have failed to grasp the nature of the illusion that is being perpetrated upon them.

The twisted 'as below—so above' thus imprints upon both the universe and the minds of people, the alien construct, stolen and perverted from the original untarnished cosmic blueprint: 'as above—so below'.

In building the new society which is our imperative, we will have to recognise and reinstate the true order of things. The one that reflects a universal cosmic order freed from the twisted clutches of the deviants.

An order manifest through our deepest intuition and guided by our highest intention. Yes, that is indeed our path and our imperative.

At War

The gender ending agenda ...or the de-sexing of man and woman

"To those who are entrained to oppose, repress and suffocate the life force which stands behind Creation, sexuality is indeed dangerous."

The Universe is sexual. Electric. Sexual-electric. Its electricity produced by a state of polarity. Polarity which causes friction. Friction as the fundamental life force. The life force which catalyses birth. Birth: an act of procreation; 'pro-creation'. A Divine act. The birthing of the Universe as Divine Action.

An action brought about by the mutual attraction existing between two interconnected, gravity-enhanced polar opposites. Negative/positive; day/night; yin/yang; male/female. No life without duality. No duality without polarity. No birth without duality/polarity. No evolution without procreation, and no procreation without the sexes.

Sexuality is sacred, an eternal fountain of the profoundly creative: therefore, in a monotone world, where survival depends upon materialistic uniformity of thought and sterile conformity of inaction, sexuality is dangerous. That danger has led to an attempt to neuter our electrically charged reality, and render obsolete the role of man, woman and even procreation itself—so as to make way for a robotic cyber-race and subsequent transhumanist takeover of this planet.

Let us explore this phenomenon further. Let us bring it to the light of day so that all shall see, and cease to deny, what stands behind the glorious actuality of life, death and universal movement. And at the same time, to recognise the existence and manifestation of a cruel master plan, to block and set in reverse this great unfolding adventure: the evolution of Life.

To those who are entrained to oppose, repress and suffocate the life force which stands behind Creation, sexuality is indeed dangerous. Especially so, since it is aligned with the birth of new life, a vessel and messenger of universal spiritual creativity.

The forces that take fright from this energetic expression of creative freedom, are aligned with an opposing state of existence. One that, in the context of this chapter, we will call 'anti-creation'. A force that seeks to subsume creative energy and invert it into its opposite. In the last chapter I identified such a force as being associated with the deception of the non-human Archons.

However, those earthly 'human' beings (and the Archontic entities that possess them) do not oppose the existence of electric energy per se. They do not wish to destroy that which provides them with the fuel needed to carry through their master plan. But they do wish to gain control over it and use it for their own ends. Not for pro-creation, but for its opposite—anti-creation, a form of life abortion.

They wish to possess that which is pure, claiming unto themselves such untainted energies, and using them as ammunition within an unquenchable ambition for power, possession and absolute dominance.

This form of power comes without empathy, compassion or love. It is hard, cold and often ruthless. It can murder, maim and eviscerate life with seemingly cool disdain.

To warm, red-blooded humans, it seems almost inconceivable. Almost inconceivable that there could be an entity devoid of these instincts; one supported (worshipped) by human beings keen to emulate its cold, robotic machismo.

But amongst what are referred to as 'the 1%', such beings are indeed to be found. For example, those who practice paedophilia and child sacrifice, while holding high office in government, banking, law, media and other similar professions. In other words, none other than those who run the day-to-day life of this planet.

It is within the ambition of such people, to support external and extra-dimensional forces that wish to take control of human DNA, while confining humanity to playing out a slavish role in support of the 'anti-creation master plan'.

Great swaths of humanity cannot (or do not wish to) believe that such entities—and the earthly beings who emulate them— actually exist and engage in such heinous acts of violence on the young and innocent who walk amongst us.

Most of the inhabitants of planet Earth cannot see that they are under the spell of a global indoctrination agenda. And that this agenda is the dominant controlling mechanism of this neo-liberal corporate era.

We who can see this reality, are here to help change that situation.

Let us draw breath a moment and ask: how is the subversion and inversion of natural sexuality actually achieved here on planet Earth? Given that it is a key element of the anti-creation mission, what is the methodology being applied to ensure its widespread adoption?

Let me start the answer to this question by reminding us that the uncorrupted nature of human and universal sexuality is spiritual in nature. We are blessed with this power. The power of procreation. This I explained in an earlier chapter: "Original Sin—A Myth Whose Time is Up".

Every male is in part, also female. Every female is in part, also male. We recognise these qualities in ourselves. They allow both sexes to empathise with each other. They are distinctive, yet entirely interconnected. Looked at dynamically, they are engaged in a Flamenco-like dance of magnetic attraction within each one of us; just as they are between us. Love starts within.

As outlined at the beginning, sexuality (sex-duality) is the essential driving force of universal life. Of movement, change, evolution. Without the 'friction' stemming from the attraction of complementary opposites, living energy-matter would never have come into existence. The source of sexuality (sex-duality) is therefore sacred.

What the anti-creation doctrine aims to do, in order to achieve its goal, is to prize apart these two lovers and make them appear to be at odds with each other. To make natural duality appear to be a conflict rather than a resolution. Distorting and contorting that which is whole so that it seems like two opposing elements.

One 'anti-creation' solution would appear to be perfecting the watering down and morphing into each other of these two states, so that they no longer appear to be distinct, but indistinct and almost entirely lacking in definition. In effect, sterilising, homogenising and neutering them. Collapsing the divine natural polarity. To make what is innately sexual – sexless. Devoid of dignity, meaning, nuance and attraction.

Another route, also being practised at this time, is to go the opposite way and overtly sexualise sex. Make it the 'in your face' titillating temptation of the moment; the 'sin' which is now on sale, or free, if you should 'get lucky'. Witness how the entertainment industry has capitalised on this vogue and pushed it down our throats with the help of such pop icons as Madonna, Lady Gaga and Miley Cyrus. All of whom have garbed themselves in Satanic robes and Saturnian symbols, blatantly conveying the source of their warped sexuality.

Such idols are adored by millions of young fans—and so the disease spreads.

The crudification of sexuality de-spiritualises its essence. This is exactly what the anti-creation agenda is all about. Either make it an amorphous void or a denatured pseudo-erotic charge. Each achieves the same aim: the deliberate distortion of the higher powers with which mankind is blessed.

Don't think that religion is free of these machinations. It is deeply immersed in such practices. One need only count the number of scandals involving priests molesting young boys and girls to know how, in too many cases, fickle and false is the supposed commitment to genuinely higher teaching in these institutions.

In the world of aspirants to spiritual enlightenment, there is a strong tendency towards sublimation of the sexual energies in favour of increasing spiritual energies. But this is an error, as they are not separate entities in the first place. They are one energy, with a plethora of colourful expressions.

The sinister pedestal upon which sit the anti-creation cabal, is not threatened by this form of sublimated aspiration, because such sublimation is itself denaturing nature and thereby draining the life-force of its vital ingredients. In fact, the act of rendering separate that which is whole, plays directly into the hands of the anticreation forces.

There is much confusion about this amongst New Age and similar spirit-oriented movements; and confusion is a tool for breaking apart the bonds of natural cohesion. Exactly what is 'meant' to happen. Many aspirants believe it goes against their belief to confront the perpetrators of evil on this planet. No wonder the cabal gets its way. No wonder the few find little resistance to their domination over the many.

Aspiration directed to Divine is a 'sexual' / 'electric' awakening. Just as the joyous act of sexual union is a 'spiritual' awakening. They are each, both. That is the great conundrum of life which so many fail to grasp. Yet grasp it we must if we are to win back our true selves and overthrow our anti-creation oppressors. The masters of divide and conquer.

Closely related to the process of human debasement is the mass denaturing of the human diet: food. Here is where genetically modified seeds/foods make their appearance. They are tools of sterility. In laboratory experiments carried out in France in 2012, rats fed GMO animal feed became incapable of reproducing after two years. They became sterile.

In addition, toxic agrichemicals, monocultural farming practices and a corporate-owned globalised food industry, have reduced the nutritional value of our daily staple foods to virtually the same level as the packets they come in. Supermarket sales propaganda has drawn billions into a world of fake food and failing health. And it's all deliberate.

Genetic engineering plant life to become an agent in the prevention of procreation, involves a blatant tampering with the gene pool upon which all life depends. It is part of the same game as the gender-bending I'm describing in this article.

The process of degradation seeps in everywhere, including language, politics, sports, education, leisure and even in simple domesticity. It's inescapably present on billboards, TV screens and cinemas from one end of the world to the other. And it's all part of a deliberate plan to undermine the organic life flow common to nature, man and the universe.

A Polish colleague, on a trip to the doctor recently, was told at the commencement of the signing-in session "I'm afraid I have to ask you what sex you are". Afraid indeed. There's talk on a number of fronts these days of making communication between the sexes 'gender neutral' so as to avoid politically incorrect discrimination... what insanity!

When things get hidden away that should be out in the public arena, then fear of touching on something that is 'not meant' to be raised, grows exponentially. Thus, polite or convivial conversations cannot include that which the status quo deems 'incorrect'. Under these circumstances one soon finds oneself in a kind of absurd conversational void where it is considered irresponsible to say almost anything remotely meaningful!

Here we have an insidious sterilisation of social intercourse. Political correctness based on 'fear'. The fear of being different, of being outside the norm. It's yet another kind of desert, a similar one to the agricultural monoculture which provides the global food market. Language reduced to a tiny fraction of what it can convey. A form of social engineering 'par excellence'.

This is a place where true communication—from the heart, soul and spirit—has been rendered as near as being taboo. Ostracised and flattened out like so much garbage on the way to the recycling station.

I really can't begin to do justice to the dastardly levels of blood-letting to which our creative, animated powers of communication have been subjected; dumbed-down at the hands of the anti-creation centralised control system that dominates this planet. A control system which goes under such titles as government, religion, commission, corporation, university, medicine, military and media.

But 'we the people' have a horrible way of falling in line with this covert and overt social engineering agenda. Many of us who should know better.

A ubiquitous example is the seemingly innocuous nonchalantly executed expression 'you guys'. Or "Hi guys!" All dignity and natural pride gone in an instant, as the sacred female and sacred male are casually deflated into a homophobic expression of that which, until recently, was considered as referring exclusively to the male of the species: 'a guy'. No longer. Now women are men too. We're all 'guys'. It doesn't matter. It's cool. It's 'non-discriminatory'. Yea, of course. To call a man a man and a woman a woman is discriminatory... sorry, I forgot.

So we're all just sexless or unisex or non-gender engendered, neutralised creatures, scared out of their wits of that which is sacred about our femaleness and maleness. About the superb electromagnetic distinctiveness inherent in sexuality. That which mirrors the divine duality of our Universe.

'As above—so below', my friends. It's time to be true to who you are. Who we are. And I countenance you from the bottom of my heart not to fall into the trap of degrading and diminishing all that which is at the vital core of our uniquely complementary differences.

You see, that is exactly what the anti-creation agenda is intended to achieve. Its executives know that once the magnetic power of the divine dance of duality is weakened to the point where the internal nucleus falls out of dynamic with its tightly packed whirling electron counterpart(s) (lovers), then that which catalyses the centrifugal expansion of the universe, is immediately in crisis.

"You guys", as innocuous as it sounds, is a prescient example of that imminent crisis.

If the subtly ecstatic tension at the heart of our electric universe is no longer brought into play on Earth (as above—so below) we earthlings will be complicit in the diminishment, not just of our own lives, but of all life. Macrocosm and microcosm are entirely complementary reflections of each other (as above—so below). We affect the evolution of the cosmos just as it affects us. That divine dance is quite simply what our innate human potentiality is continuously reaching towards the full expression of, here on Earth.

The degree of its manifestation (art) marks the degree of our creative development and expressiveness. The various degrees of manifest creative expression set the agenda for the ongoing evolution of all humanity.

We would seem to be on a knife edge between breakthrough and breakdown. Maybe that sounds unduly optimistic, because the breakdown is all too evident and the breakthrough much less so. However, what is visible represents a tiny fraction of what exists, in this universe, so we should not let it dominate our mood.

It is said that 'the darkest hour is just before dawn', so that when pressed hard against the wall beyond which we cannot go, we discover the existence of strengths we didn't realise we possessed.

Mankind, while seemingly cast asunder by the deliberately engineered chaos of the anti-creation agenda, is actually simultaneously moving closer to a state of dynamic unity, at the unseen deeper level. All attempts to render the distinctive—indistinct; the deep—superficial; the divine—satanic; the full—empty; are forcing into the open that which has the power to reverse this great oppression and redeem the glory of life.

It is a critical moment of great drama in the affairs of man and the universe. A moment in which truth can be seized with both hands and carried forward. Carried forward in the spirit of joyously offering back a precious gift to the source from which all life was made manifest. Returning something, which, out of fear and selfishness, we wished to keep only for ourselves; and in so doing, distorted beyond recognition.

Once the gift of Life is celebrated as the unique treasure it truly is, a great cry of thanks spontaneously rises within us, echoing out as a healing wave into the greater spheres of existence. And at this very same moment, the messengers and instigators of anti-creation are blown backwards, losing their grip and their domination over those who have for so long acted as fuel for their parasitic existence.

Yes, it is our imperative—and ours only—to rid the universe of these agents of destruction. We were imbued with the ability to perform this act and we must now go boldly forward to achieve it. Yes, good friends, we are so close to this great day—yet so far if we insist on denial. If we insist on denial of our innate duality. If we refuse to extol the beauty of the two great archetypal lovers; if we refuse to participate in the great dance of life.

Participate now, or depart this life as a mere shadow of your real self; an amorphous void in a sexless universe.

Seize the great moment. For its wealth and beauty hovers so tantalisingly within the grasp of every woman and every man willing to fully embrace the joyous gift of Life.

The madness of war

It is essential to constantly remind ourselves, that war, apart from a very few exceptions, is a symptom of madness.

Yet war is a disease which is largely taken for granted; considered 'normal' and unless it involves a large swath of humanity, ignored. How did we allow ourselves to be trapped by such insanity?

Wars are as prevalent as ever. They are being manifest in the Middle East, in Africa, in South America, and in a lesser form, in almost all countries of the World. They are the result of a failure to recognise that killing another is actually killing one's self. A failure to grasp that humanity is a collective made up of millions of individuals, all of whom share a common ancestry and, on a subconscious level, a common aspiration and destiny.

There is no victory in war. War is an admission of defeat. When humans resort to mass killing of each other we see an expression of failure, never success. Not so long ago war was glorified and, for the victor, held up as an expression of supreme national pride. In fact, such an attitude was predominant in the species for thousands of years.

However, two World Wars put an end to this hubris. The levels of destruction were so great and so many millions died brutal and ugly deaths, that a kind of 'war weariness' set in amongst the survivors, and a new sense of the futility of it all became integrated into societies which had undergone the experience. The world looked as if it might have learned its lesson; people had pounded each other—and the natural environment— into a sickening pulp, and there was no glorious aftermath. Just some sense of what 'peace' could actually mean.

There were—and are—still some who find war 'exciting', whose own lives are too dull and routine to find any thrill in the act of daily living. They are lookers-on at wars in foreign territories as extensions of their own angst and frustrations. Such individuals find temporary comfort in watching others die.

This condition is more prevalent than many might realise; it is symptomatic of a world crushed by meaningless routine and managed by those lacking any manifest vision of something more deeply fulfilling to awaken starved imaginations.

Of course, a history of war will reveal that whole civilisations were born and dissolved via victory and defeat on the battlefield. It was believed that these blood-baths were a price worth paying for the great accumulation of national wealth which followed them—if one was on the winning side. It is sobering to reflect that much of the fine architecture of old Europe is a result of plundered wealth.

War is made no less destructive by the fact that it can now be carried out by people sitting in air conditioned 'cockpits' in Houston. People trained to kill 'at a distance'. People whose chance of being themselves attacked by those they target, being pretty much nil. This type of killing is one step away from the 'robotic soldier', the envisioned battlefield of the future and a direct extension of the war games kids (and adults) play on their electronic gizmos.

But look, it's still the same underlying disease. It's still the fascination with the idea of somehow 'coming out on top' and having it over 'an inferior'. It's still revelling in destruction, on all levels of planetary life.

Children play war games. I used to play 'Cowboys and Indians'. I was indoctrinated into 'war thinking' from a very early age. It was just after World War II, and life in Britain was steeped in stories of heroism carried out by 'our boys' against the Nazis. Toy soldier armies ranged against each other across the sitting room floor as parents looked on with quiet acceptance. We soon graduated on to 'cap guns' and staged mock battles around the garden bushes and trees.

But nobody got killed in these 'war games' and the ground wasn't turned into a sea of craters and toxic mud by our childhood antics. Other matters eventually attracted our curiosity and interest, and the guns and bows and arrows were dumped, unlikely to be seen again.

If mankind would only grow up, the same situation would be repeated around the world. Adult individuals, blessed with a little responsibility and the slimmest glimmer of wisdom, would 'move on' to areas of interest that expressed an eagerness to support the planet, and not destroy it. A wish to explore new horizons of consciousness, and not to regress into thoughtless thuggery. A desire to meet and enjoy the company of other races and nationalities, and not to put a gun to their heads.

How can this madness have gone on so long? How can war still 'be taken for granted' in the twenty-first century?

Even those who argue vociferously for cutting back excessive CO_2 emissions on the planet, don't call for an end to war and 'war games' that are responsible for a large part of these emissions. They fail to realise that here is to be found the single largest transmission of toxic CO_2 when set against any other global activity. I'm including a brief summary of the US position in 2013, just to illustrate the point:

"According to its own study, in 2013 the Pentagon consumed fuel equivalent to 90,000,000 barrels of crude oil. This amounts to 80% of the total fuel usage by the federal government. If burned as jet fuel it produces about 38,700,000 metric tons of CO_2. And the Pentagon's figures do not include carbon produced by the thousands of bombs dropped in 2013, or the fires that burned after the jets and drones departed." (Counter Punch).

Most environmentalists and climate change campaigners also 'take war for granted', it seems. It has been etched into our bones by an endless indoctrination process. A process whose symptoms can also be found in the way we are urged to be 'aggressive' and 'competitive' in order to make progress within the demands of the status quo. How much of what is called 'education' is about bringing out our creative potential instead of our aggressive potential? And how much is about cramming us with the means to 'succeed' in the mostly cutthroat world of business and indeed, almost all professions?

We see the symptoms of aggression in daily life, and fail to question it. Is it any wonder that we fail to question war?

War is the most favoured tool of the controlling powers. It supplies the coffers of the military-industrial complex with an endless demand for production of weapons. The state then gets the payoff and looks for another war to keep the cycle of death going. It is also a valuable diversionary tool for distracting the general public, while unpopular and controversial issues are pushed through the system, with only a few noticing.

Of course, a great prize for warmongers in general, is anticipation of the breaking out of mother of all wars. And indeed, the ever-looming threat of genocide never seems far off at the hands of those who play with power the way children play with their toy guns and swords, but without any of the child's creativity.

Today, in the USA in particular, megalomania has become wedded with a sort of Russian roulette approach to who might present the next useful target for a bombing run or drone attack.

Witness how high the stakes get set in this fiendish game. Witness the Russian Federation and President Putin being ever further provoked by the West to take an aggressive step that could trigger a mega war scenario. The vicious taunting, without a shred of evidence to give it credence, is a mark of the madness which all too often grips those in power. Those who are determined to diminish all of life to a poisoned arrow of fabricated fear, which, if ever launched, would take all of humanity with it.

Let us be sure to keep a close eye on those whom we elect to administer our countries. The intoxication which comes with power is a very dangerous addiction, particularly when the playthings at such people's disposal are weapons of mass destruction. We need, more than ever, to be able to recognise the symptoms of megalomania and not confuse it with 'strong leadership'. It is a major weakness in the delivery of what is called democracy, that so many people are still so easily fooled by those standing for election.

We are being pushed by 'anti-life' forces, some of whose

origins are less than human, to see the planet and its people as expendable. To accept lies, deception and crude power-play as something akin to 'normal'. To feel that it is not in our powers to bring deep change to a washed-out and degraded status quo. To believe that war is an acceptable way of shifting around the totems of power.

It's time we not only woke up, but got out of bed too. The hour is late, and this should add a significant degree of urgency to our endeavours. Mankind is blessed with deep powers of positive potential and these powers are far greater than the force which drives the warmongering anti-life minority. We are close to a tipping point in the growth of conscious awareness amongst caring human beings.

The key will be to channel this awareness into taking measures to regain control of our destinies.

To rid this world of those who hold its fate in their numb, insensitive hands. To act in unison and to defy all efforts to divide and conquer our growing sense of purpose and endeavour.

We can, and we will, put an end to the madness of war. We must not wait for war to put an end to us.

Collectively realised creation versus mutually assured destruction

This title speaks to the opposing ambitions of two forces at large on our planet. Those which work towards the realisation of a great vision—and those which work towards the annihilation of all vision.

Although they stand at diametrically opposite extremes in the process we call 'life', their presence is increasingly felt within the everyday workings of our planet.

The concept of 'collectively realised creation' is rooted in the collective unconscious of humanity. In all of us. It is that which informs our desire to live and to outwardly express that desire. To express it through actions that reflect the depth and wealth of the creative sparks within each one of us.

Whereas 'mutually assured destruction' (MAD)—a term used to describe the East-West 'Cold War' nuclear missile build-up of the 1980s—has no part in the human script; but is nevertheless a state towards which our planet is being pushed by forces that appear blind to their own madness. But then perhaps madness cannot ever recognise itself.

As it is, it has turned out not to be that hard to set humanity rushing off in the opposite direction from that which informs the flowering of collectively realised creation. All it took was the devising of a confidence trick to make us humans feel guilty about that which fulfils our simple heartfelt joys.

Once successfully seeded, the relentless stoking of this 'guilt/ fear' confidence trick, caused it to take a stronger and stronger hold on the psyche of humanity, until the great majority had taken it upon themselves to purchase an insurance policy with 'Mutual Assured Destruction plc'.

An insurance policy guaranteed to so deaden the voice of the natural life force that Collectively Realised Creation could no longer make itself heard—or barely.

MAD soon became a monopoly, a mutual insurance company with a global membership far exceeding any similar outfit.

However, sometimes some of its clients still inadvertently feel an unpleasant twinge of consciousness. A brief painful glimpse of truth, whose origin is usually traced back to Collectively Realised Creation. This pain is very irksome, so its sufferers rush to put in a claim with MAD, which after all, guaranteed protection against the promptings of truth.

MAD is generous in this—it pays out—as well as offering its claimants further protection free of charge! Its happy clients head at once to the glittering arcade for their brand new flat screen TV, microwave and iPod. The zombie purchaser does not see, of course, that each purchase provides further fuel to the sycophantic ambitions of Mutually Assured Destruction.

It is no surprise that MAD has become somewhat bloated on the poisoned fruits its own success. A success unprecedented, not only amongst other 'mutuals', but amongst multinational corporations in general. In fact, sensing the opportunity to still further increase its empire, MAD recently brokered a deal with the architects of 'Full Spectrum Dominance'. And in a wedding made in hell, the satanic duo headed out to silence, once and for all, the never entirely repressible energies of Collectively Realised Creativity.

The Full Spectrum Dominance school of top-down control has long since been interested in the complete transcendence of limitations. That is "getting beyond gender, law, nature and time and space" (John Dyer). They are the people behind the establishment of the world's vast trading blocs, the Agenda 21 scam, smart grids, biochemical weapons and the push towards a progressive takeover by artificial intelligence—the transhumanist agenda.

They are Bilderberger emanations; the architects of TTIP, NAFTA, the military-industrial complex and the deliberate fermentation of world wars. The full realisation of their game is the establishment of a One World Government.

But these dark agendas used to be hidden. They were fermented in great secrecy; they were known only to a few. They were subject to Masonic and Jesuit blood oaths of obedience 'not to tell'. But all this has changed. I wouldn't be writing these words if the knowledge and exposé of these agendas weren't rapidly gathering momentum; if a broad awakening wasn't well under way.

So it is, that in this 21st century, our blessed planet Earth has become the theatre for a mighty show-down between diametrically opposed forces: those of Collectively Realised Creation and those of Mutually Assured Destruction. Utterly antithetical visions of the future, increasingly played out in the here and now.

There can be little doubt that the bloated over-confidence of MAD is currently suffering incessant puncturing by the bright arrows of collective truth. The entire empire of what we know as 'the status quo' is rocking on its hinges and the door marked PTB threatens to become entirely unhinged.

Collectively Realised Creation is gaining in self-confidence daily. She is staging a major comeback, and MAD knows it. That is why this is such a pivotal time for us all. For planet Earth, its animals, trees, rivers and seas.

Within the volcanic eruptions that manifest themselves with ever greater frequency, a symbol of yet greater eruption can be felt. A trembling in the air and at the very depths of existence. A huge metamorphosis rising ever closer to the surface of all human affairs. Birth pains of the world to come.

We should expect the unexpected in apocalyptic times like these.

As things get increasingly brittle, pipes burst, electric circuits fuse, and people lose their marbles.

Unconstrained acts of savagery and torture stage their pentup violence, openly. Mind controlled mental cases go on the rampage. While the sons and daughters of millionaire bankers sip champagne on ice in six star hotel bars, millions face starvation in foreign deserts of exploitation.

It's all up on the screen now, in fifty shades of red and green.

Yet, simultaneous to these manifest scenes of destruction, are scenes speaking boldly of creation. Of the building of unity around great humanitarian initiatives. Of overcoming the torment of weaknesses that provide ready fuel for the vampiric MAD to so avidly gorge itself.

It is here, amongst the rising Phoenix of awakening, that we belong. We who feel the sap rising in our salty veins, who sense the powerful portent in the great showdown of diametrically opposite intents now engulfing humanity, demanding an unwavering answer to the ever-prescient question: 'to be or not to be'?

But we know that in truth—there is no 'choice'. For we are a Collective Force of Creativity. It is we, the people, who are awakening from our prolonged and listless sleep.

Yes, and it's a seriously rude awakening. Because after wiping the sleep from our eyes, we find ourselves looking straight down the barrel of nothing less than MAD's merciless machine gun— which will surely fire us—should we fail to rise up as one, to this, our final call.

The global warming matrix

In the last two decades, in particular, we have been confronted by a climatologist information tsunami. It started with the announcement that something called 'The Greenhouse Effect' was at work on a global level; an unwelcome warming purported to be the result of 'greenhouse gases', most notably CO_2-linked to the industrial revolution and subsequent industrial and transportation developments across the globe.

The term 'Greenhouse Effect' then faded out, to be replaced by the term 'Global Warming'. This took a rather broader sweep in describing a warming trend also exacerbated by emissions like methane and nitrous oxides, as well as problems associated with an increase in acidification of the oceans. But things got a lot more complex around the year 2000 when the term 'Climate Change' then usurped its predecessor's place.

Climate Change introduces a far wider remit to the whole equation, greatly broadening the potential terms of reference of the debate. The term, one can hardly fail to observe, sheds any mention of 'warming'. Now climatologists and government were given license to state: "We may have been wrong about the warming effects, but we were right about climate change".

Controversy Everywhere…

Controversy had already surrounded the various prognoses of The Intergovernmental Panel on Climate Change established by the United Nations to deal with slowing the rate of global warming. Amongst other things, climatologists struggled to agree upon how many parts per million of atmospheric CO_2 constituted a red line beyond which one dared not go. They even fiddled the figures in an attempt to make the reality fit the prognosis.

In the meantime, the 'green movement' seized upon CO_2 emission increases, and vigorously proposed a renewable 'clean energy' solution capable of providing adequate energy for all, at very little cost to the environment and biosphere.

The political implications of devising an energy strategy capable of satisfying the climatologists, the corporations (upon which government finances heavily depend and the vociferous Greens, took on an ever-greater significance.

The battle-lines were drawn: would climate change become the biggest single catalyst for rethinking and reworking centuries of reliance on carbon emitting fossil fuels, mined at ever greater depths, so as to keep the globalised market place chundering onwards, forever eviscerating the sacred sites of nature's diminishing untainted canvas? Or would the whole thing be fudged?

Al Gore's leap to pre-eminence as the seer of climatic Armageddon was followed by other famous entertainers, sporting instantly acquired green credentials. The NASA space agency also got in on the act, pushing forward its own take of the state of play. A few eminent detractors held out with a very different prognosis on the science, which rapidly earned them the title of 'deniers'. Nevertheless, we were required to face the possibility that dear old Earth might actually be moving into a phase of global cooling, not warming at all.

That pretty much brings us to where we are today. For us Westerners, ever greater swaths of giant wind turbines and banks of solar panels bear testimony to the political credence given to the favoured scientific prognosis: that CO_2 and other related particulate emissions must be kept below the red line of 400 parts per million.

The Greens eulogise about the numbers of jobs that this 'green revolution' will create, while nobody seems to want an eighty metre wind turbine near their second, or even first home. Nor has the embedded energy involved in constructing all these turbines ever been seriously assessed.

But all this might still just about pass for some degree of progress on the road to a greener, cleaner world...if it were not for one or two areas of absolute denial that present a great schism in the overall scheme of things. Areas of denial which have the effect of raising a large question mark about the authenticity of the entire process.

The first missing link is the fact that it is 'war' which produces the single greatest volume of man-made CO_2 emission on this planet. It is the vast military-industrial complex which stands behind the preeminence of the global market place and neo-liberal capitalism itself, that exceeds any other single activity on Earth in contributing to climatologists' views on what is causing climate change.

Have you ever heard military exercises and war being raised as the major cause of man-made climate change? Not likely. No, that is taboo. Not just in governmental circles, but in fact in about every institution concerned with climate change, including the Greens.

To leave the war machine out of the picture renders highly questionable the entire motivation behind correcting the consensus-backed causes of climate change. It is taboo, because the great majority of consensus supporters are part and parcel of an economic system whose roots—and wealth—are dependent upon the vast financial earnings derived from arms sales and the military industrial machine. A machine whose engines are kept turning 24/7 by vast volumes of carbon sucked up and mined from beneath the Earth's surface. And that, it seems, is very unwelcome news.

The general exclusion from public debate of the military's role in raising global emission levels, is indicative of a grand scale cover-up which must be laid bare if any genuine progress in planetary healing is to be made.

Please try to consider the implications of 'the denial of war' on the way our society operates today. The taking for granted of that which brings havoc and misery wherever it is perpetrated and just happens to spew millions of tons of noxious elements into the atmosphere at the same time. Manifest madness.

Ecocide or we decide?

When you take a closer look at it, you see that the choices we make each day of our lives add up to the grand price that nature must pay in her role as the sustainer of life on this planet.

What do I mean by that?

Well, it's simple enough: if we choose to live a life of inverted personal self-interest and unawareness; of disregard for nature and of disinterest in the effect our actions have on the greater socio-economic environment around us, then we are playing our part in the trashing of this planet, its animals, insects, fish, rivers, seas, soils, atmosphere and peoples. But that's not all, we are also playing a part in trashing our own nature—that potentiality to grow—which is our absolute birthright and common imperative. So, if we decide that we don't want to grow, we are destined to contribute to the deficit of the resource base of the planet. By not consciously acting to support life we become complicit in acting against it. There can be no other conclusion. No halfway house. So, once having committed to give support to that which enhances life on earth, it soon becomes clear that a great swath of our society's daily preoccupations is working in opposition to this commitment. Going against the laws of nature. Going against that which holds the promise of a future for us all.

Can life go on this way indefinitely?

No, it can't. We already have evidence that if the southern hemisphere of the planet chose to achieve the same 'standard of living' as most of the northern hemisphere, we would need five more planet Earths to sustain ourselves. We don't have five more planet Earths—and even if we did—carrying on in the same way as now simply means we would ultimately trash all of them!

We are living beyond our means. We are sucking at the bosom of an under-nourished resource and appear incapable of weaning ourselves off its precious milk. That's a pretty shocking weakness. When a calf grows up, the mother kicks the impudent youngster for still attempting to grab her teats—and that's what mother nature ultimately does to us if we refuse to grow up and wake up.

How can we wake up when all around us others are sleeping on the job?

Answer: set the alarm—and when it rings, get out of bed. Don't be sidelined by others who sleep on. Focus on what really matters and take that road to work. Avoid the mega-highway—it leads over a cliff and to the extinction of the human race.

You see, we need to be genuinely conscious of the results of our actions. There's a ton of information out there now, telling just how to lighten our ecological footprint on this beleaguered planet. How to tread softly in the moccasin; to counteract the stamp of the jack-boot.

However, the deficit side has some pretty powerful drugs to keep us asleep... to stop us hearing the alarm. In fact, it has a masterful way of keeping us in a state of funk because it controls the education system of the Western World and most of the rest as well. It uses cunning and guile to make us believe that education is about conforming to a plan that will drop us off the end of the production line as a 'ready slave' for something called 'the job market'. And it's this 'job market' that is largely dependent for its existence on trashing the world's resources.

So you see, you land up in a rapidly stagnating cul-de-sac. Nowhere to go except around and around in ever diminishing circles. Education is not education—it is indoctrination. Welcome to the brave new world of centralised control and Orwellian dystopia. Real education starts when you get off the treadmill and cut loose.

How can I get 'a real education'?

I'll tell you: by deciding to decide what's best for you – and aligning that decision with what's best for planet Earth.

'Education' comes from the Latin word 'e-ducare' meaning 'to lead out from'. Yes exactly! To lead out from, not to 'push into'. Once that inner potential is sparked one's real education begins and all that which is good in us, nay great, can eventually be led out and find its place in that which turns the fortunes of this planet around.

Now, finding one's niche and finding one's self are pretty much synonymous. So, the question jumps up: how can I avoid contributing to the deficit side while heading out on this new journey?

This is a crucial question, for it is all too easy to land up in a no-man's-land. Two steps forward, two steps back. So I propose courage as the first essential ingredient. Then I propose acquiring a skill that will help you to be more independent, more capable of taking control of your own destiny—both now—and when the lights go out. That means some real hands-on work experience. A grounding in the practical. That which puts the academic and mind laden school and university curriculum in proper perspective.

Something that challenges another part of your body. That arouses another part of your being. That which puts you in touch with the reality of life for billions of self-sufficient and semi self-sufficient communities all over this world; as well as with an increasing number of innovative young people looking to broaden their horizons, grow their own foods, build their homes, develop skills of the land. The wind is blowing this way now. Listen to it and move with it.

It's not about 'making money', but making a fresh start. A fresh start in a way of life that does not trash the planet, but rather contributes to its emancipation and amelioration. A way of life which can open one's soul to the pull of nature, one's hands to contact with the soil and the tools of the artisan. For if we are to be against ecocide, we need also to be for life. That demands action.

Technocracy, Globalisation and Totalitarianism

Closing the gate on GMO and the criminal TTIP

"What emerges is an understanding of TTIP as the political project of a transatlantic corporate and political elite which, on the unfounded promise of increased trade and job creation, will attempt to reverse social and environmental regulatory protections, redirect legal rights from citizens to corporations, and consolidate US and European global leadership in a changing world order." (Seattle to Brussels Network)

A key element of this Transatlantic Trade Agreement, but only one of hundreds of highly controversial proposals, is the move to deregulate the status currently accorded to imports of GM seeds and plants for cultivating in European soils.

A determined effort by all of us, who care about real food and real farming, will be needed to stop one of the most insidious attempts yet to end Europe's widespread resistance to genetically modified organisms. In particular, the use of GM seeds in European agriculture, leading to genetically modified crops being grown in areas that have, up until now, successfully resisted the GM corporate invasion.

The EU has so far licensed just one GM maize variety (MON 810) to be grown within its territories, and one potato variety (Amflora) for industrial starch production. Up until now, the EU has acted according to a largely restrictive trade practice concerning GM and other controversial food products due to major public pressure, as well as under a broad EU ruling termed 'the precautionary principle'.

All that could be about to go out the window under negotiations between the USA and the European Commission to ratify a new trade agreement known as TTIP, the Transatlantic Trade and Investment Partnership. Don't be fooled by the current attempts to explain things away; the deals will be struck behind our backs if they can't be achieved under the spotlight of public interest.

The objective of this 'partnership' is to facilitate far going corporate control of the international market place and to prize open the mostly closed (but not locked) European door on GM crops and seeds.

While this corporate heist is being eased into place, replicas have been negotiated between Canada and the EU under the title 'Comprehensive Economic Trade Agreement', CETA. And as if that wasn't enough, a further dismantling of trade tariffs is underway via the 'Trade In Services Agreement', TiSA: a wide-ranging further liberalisation of corporate trading conditions as a direct continuation of the WTO (World Trade Organisation) GATS agreement, with its highly onerous, corporate biased 'Codex Alimentarius' sanitary and hygiene rulings. Indigenous seeds and medicinal herbs are particularly under attack via Codex.

We can thus recognise, from the outset, that a very dangerous interference of the already leaky checks and balances that control the import/export market is underway here. The thinly disguised under-text reveals plans for a massive corporate takeover of all negotiated quasi-democratic trade agreements and food quality controls that currently take place between the US and the EU. It is clear that the major corporate concerns are determined to overcome or dilute all resistance to their unfettered 'free trade' goals.

Where they are blocked, corporations are claiming the right to sue governments and institutions held to be 'infringing the principle of international free trade'. Such litigation procedures are not new, but the idea of writing them into a major trading agreement has sparked major controversy. For example, in Germany, where one of the main Swedish nuclear power construction companies sued the German government for billions of euros, with the intention of gaining full compensation for the ban on nuclear power enacted earlier by the Merkel government.

To add a further sinister twist to this already draconian exercise in power politics, the court hearings on such actions are slated to take place in secret, in a court house in Washington DC. Such secret courts are already operational in the UK, where 'sensitive cases' can be heard out of sight of public scrutiny with no reports or summaries of the proceedings released into the public domain. Here we witness the Orwellian control system fully up and running, with its attendant undisguised destruction of many decades of hard-won civil liberties.

The unremitting and relentless nature of this neo-capitalist and corporate centralisation of power is causing significant resistance to manifest itself: Millions have galvanised themselves into action to block the advance of this behemoth.

For the purpose of this summary, I am not able to cover the full gamut of trading controversies being brought to a head by the ongoing negotiations, preferring to concentrate on the food and farming implications. But it is very important not to lose sight of the true intention behind all aspects of these nefarious trade agreements.

As a precursor to TTIP, a major shift in GMO legislation was already voted in by the EU's Environmental Council on 12 June 2014. After many years of EU member state disagreement on GM issues—leading to negotiation stalemate—this controversial agreement devolves GMO decision-making procedures from Brussels to EU member states.

In the process, however, it gives the green light to pro-GMO governments to allow the planting of GM crops in their countries, while anti-GM member states can put forward economic and environmental health arguments to ban GM crops. Under the first draft of this agreement, countries wishing to block GM plantings were called upon to seek permission to ban such crops from the very corporations that are proposing to introduce them! A proposal whose unprecedented arrogance echoes the corporate agenda of TTIP and CETA trade proposals.

Fortunately, after intensive public lobbying, this clause was dropped (November 11, 2014, Environment, Public Health and Food Safety Committee).

Nevertheless, what we have in front of our eyes is a strong GMO warning light. A dual alert in fact. Firstly owing to the EU Commission's devolvement of 'the right to decide' to member states, and secondly owing to the TTIP agreement, which, if ratified, would allow GM crops and seeds currently banned in Europe—as well as various medicated animal products such as US hormone enriched beef—to have a largely unrestricted flow into the EU. By-passing, in the process, the 'precautionary principle' and the European Food Safety Agency's views (for what they are worth) on the efficacy of such products.

The TTIP agreement—if fully ratified—would, in effect, remove any differences in trade related legislation between the EU and the US. In corporate speak, such differences are held up as being 'trade distorting'. TTIP could also be used to attack positive food related initiatives in the US, such as 'local preference' legislation at the state level. It calls for 'mutual recognition' between trading blocs: trade-speak for lowering standards.

Consumer groups have already pointed out that mutual recognition of standards is not an acceptable approach since it will require at least one of the parties to accept food that is not of a currently acceptable standard. To put it in simple terms: the pressure to lower standards in Europe to 're-solve the inconsistencies' will be strong, and far more likely to succeed than the other solution: to raise standards in the USA.

Phrases like 'harmonisation' and 'regulatory cooperation' are a frequently occurring part of TTIP tradespeak. But in the end it's all going one way: downwards... to the lowest common denominator. Chlorine washed factory farmed US chickens.

According to Corporate Europe Observatory:

"Under TTIP's chapter on 'regulatory cooperation' any future measure that could lead us towards a more sustainable food system, could be deemed 'a barrier to trade' and thus refused before it sees the light of day. Big business groups like Business Europe and the US Chamber of Commerce have been pushing for this corporate lobby dream scenario before the US-EU negotiations ever began. What they want from regulatory cooperation is to essentially co-write legislation and to establish a permanent EU-US dialogue to work towards harmonising standards long after TTIP has been signed. Despite earlier reservations, the Commission now seems to go along with this corporate dream. Leaked EU proposals outline a new system of regulatory cooperation between the EU and the US that will enable decisions to be made without any public oversight or engagement."

What this means is that new, highly controversial GM seed lines will have virtually no publicly scrutinised safety net to slow or halt their progress to the fields and dinner plates of Europe.

TTIP and CETA are perfect weapons for the long-planned for destruction of national sovereignty. Trade negotiators, GM exponents, big farming unions, agrichemical businesses and food processing giants are all in on the game and have strong lobby groups backing TTIP. Their view on what the word 'cooperation' means goes like this "A system of regulatory cooperation would prevent 'bad decisions'—thereby avoiding having to take governments to court later" (Corporate Europe Observatory).

These 'bad decisions' constitute any attempts by governments to rein in the overt lust for power which is the hallmark of the corporate elite. For example, biotech and pesticide giants Syngenta and Bayer, are taking the European Union to court over its partial ban on three insecticides from the Neonicotinoid family, because of their deadly impact on bees. However, let us be clear, the European Union is only acting this way because of intense public pressure to do so; left to its own devices there would be no discernible difference between it and the corporate elite who stalk the corridors of power at the European Commission and European Parliament.

The underlying goal of 'regulatory cooperation' between Big Industry and the EU, is to have a continuous 'on going' dialogue (known as 'living agreement') that could ultimately render any final TTIP agreement largely meaningless. Meaningless, because it could by-pass any failures of TTIP to gain concessions on food and environmental standards by focusing on altering 'implementation rules'—rather than taking the more arduous route of altering 'the law' itself. Tinkering with 'implementation rules' simply offers another way for corporate friendly concessions to become enshrined in common trading rights.

Reassurances from EU and US negotiators that "food standards will not be lowered" have always looked highly suspect. Farmers should be alert to the fact that, because of TTIP, imports are highly likely be allowed that do not meet local standards, thus undermining national trading disciplines.

This applies across the spectrum and includes currently non-compliant GMO. According to Corporate Europe Observatory "Regulatory convergence will fundamentally change the way politics is done in the future, with industry sitting right at the table, if they get their way."

If they get their way. Well, Trump has put a spanner in TTIP's works for now, but we must not allow ourselves to think that's the end of it. No chance. It's just a welcome, all be it temporary obstruction.

All groups and organisations that care about retaining a largely GMO Free Europe and the consumption of genuine, healthy food—in tandem with the ecological farming methods that produce it—had better stick to the task of preventing any sneaked revival of TTIP, and the other related trading proposals mentioned earlier. Because they threaten to destroy the last line of defence against a complete corporate takeover of the food chain.

Beyond a failing European superstate— deciding the future we want

This subject, already touched on earlier in 'European Superstate—One Step Closer or Imminent Collapse?' — should be of interest to everyone, regardless of where you live. We are all affected by the unravelling of this behemoth called the European Union, just as we are by its continued presence. It is, after all, a work of Mammon; yet masterfully disguised as a Pan-European socio-economic entente cordiale.

It has its roots in the historical imperative of empire-building and came into being as a direct extension of Hitler's Nazi inspired goal of establishing a 'Third Reich'.

The leading voice of the EU's first version, the European Union Treaty of 1957, was a German named Walter Hallstein. He became the founder president of the Commission of the European Economic Community and one of the founding fathers of the European Union. His suitability for filling this role was based upon his earlier work as a senior attorney of the Nazi/IG Farben partnership based in the Auschwitz concentration camp. The line of continuity is direct.

However, the blueprint that led to the formation of the European Union was first tabled at a meeting of the highly secretive Bilderberg group in Rome some four years earlier. The Bilderberg group, which meets annually to this day, is composed of elite bankers, industrialists, political high-flyers and royalty. It is hardly surprising that the notion of a European Superstate should find favour with this assembly.

We are looking at the key individuals behind what became a self-selecting, autocratic top-down hierarchy. A hierarchy whose decision-making process would be entirely self-contained. It was never, by any remotest stretch of the imagination, a 'people's movement'. Nor did it aspire to any form of democracy; but developed rapidly into a centrally based technocracy. A pyramid, whose top-end bureaucracy consists of an unelected cabal serving the interest of big business, multinational corporations and political power mongers interested in the wider control of humanity as a whole.

It is a major plank in the long desired elite vision of a 'New World Order'.

Hallstein himself stated in his book 'Europe in the Making': "The Commission is entrusted with what virtually amounts to a monopoly in taking the initiative in all matters affecting the Community. There are few exceptions to this general rule, but these ought to be removed at the earliest opportunity."

He adds: "As I see it, the Commission should eventually be empowered to take all measures necessary for the implementation of the Treaty on its own authority, without having to rely on special and specific approval by the Council of Ministers."

Thus it has been and continues to be. But due to a fundamental belief and expertise in the powers of deception, it has carried some four hundred million European citizens along with it under the aegis of uniting independent nations behind what it has claimed to be 'an economically beneficial harmonisation of rules and regulations'.

A process which has led the European Union to become the largest trading bloc in the world, with a rule book so big that nobody has ever read it. The Commission poses as a 'supranational' authority, overseeing the 'acquis communautaire' (the great acquired rule book) under which all member nation states are bound.

'Supranational': please remember that this means 'above national' the 'highest authority'—that which supersedes national law.

What an incredible feat! Millions and millions across the continent of Europe have come to passively accept the covert—and often overt—imposition of a dictatorship under the illusion that it is a benign force for good.

But such deception cannot prevail forever. Signs of dissent have been growing for decades. In 2001 the Irish voted 'no' to being party to the Nice Treaty. The news rocked Europe, causing the Commission to put the Irish government under enormous pressure to do a rerun and to embark on a massive propaganda exercise warning that the Irish economy would collapse unless it voted in favor of the Treaty. It duly conformed.

Further tremblings have grown in intensity since that time, and then, in June 2016, the infamous 'Brexit' was launched into reality. It shook the nation and it shook the federation and the shock waves have not ceased to reverberate. With similar rebellions simmering on a number of fronts throughout the Union, cracks are opening up that can no longer be papered over.

There are good reasons to be suspicious of the sincerity of the British government in genuinely freeing Britain from the chains that have bound it to the Union for the past forty four years. Too many inconsistencies litter the current negotiation process and too many unknowns face the entire project, for anyone to have much faith in the veracity of the final outcome.

Whatever the political reality actually is, one thing in particular is alarming the powers that be: People are becoming aware.

Slowly at first, but week by week the process is gathering pace.

As a result, a large question now presents itself to all citizens of Europe and beyond: what shape do we want our collective futures to take?

Do we actually have a vision of the future we want? And if not, why not?

This is not a Utopian question. Those who think it is, are unwilling to recognise the power that exists among 'we the people' to bring about the change we want to see. Not to countenance this is to remain a slave to the same control system which is suffocating the creative power at the heart of humanity.

When I speak of change, I mean real change, the clearing away of not just the EU, but all known versions of 'government' and their replacement with a new model which will rise up from the grassroots.

So to get things underway, I'm going to make my contribution by briefly outlining a vision of the general direction I believe we could and should be moving in.

Firstly, in order for EU countries and regions to (re)establish their socio-economic and cultural identity and organic sense of direction, they must actually break free from the fascistic superstate which is today's reality. Also, as I have stated above, break free from all recognised forms of top-down government, since virtually all of them are deeply corrupt and in the pockets of corporate interests. This 'ditching of the dead' is the prerogative for moving forward.

Once freed from the neo-liberal/neo-con military-industrial project covertly imposed by an alliance of US government interests, the European Commission and the governments of most Western nation states, each country will be able to once again explore its priorities and to freely redefine its relationship with its neighbours.

Right from the start, the old 'globalisation model' must be abandoned in favour of the reintegration of production and marketing according to an inter-regional and local pattern.

Supply and demand will be based upon what I have termed elsewhere as 'The Proximity Principle'. Food and farming will be geared to firstly supplying the needs of the nation, the nation's regions and the local communities of these regions. The same applies to re-establishment of national fisheries. This is supply and demand based upon actual geographic proximity rather than distorted global market priorities.

It equally applies to the demand for fuel and fibre. In my view, the production and supply of localised, renewable, ecologically sustainable sources of food, fuel and fibre, is the practical model towards which we should all be working.

It is of fundamental importance for all countries to responsibly manage their indigenous resource base before turning to distant market places for their supposed needs. That is a rule that has been broken with impunity for decades, leading to a profligate mining of global resources according to a 'market demand' that pays absolutely no attention to the environmental consequences, jobs or quality of life of those stuck on the production chain.

A second, and connected, criterion will be to enable many more people to have affordable access to productive land, so that they can support themselves by growing and processing their own food.

The old capitalist 'market economy' has bled the natural resource base almost dry right across the planet. It is a blinkered and divisive paradigm which must go. The EU's contribution has been to exploit this market economy so as to build a virtually impregnable power base for itself while simultaneously creating the largest trading block in the world.

It has tried to impose a blanket 'one system fits all' policy over a group of widely diverse nations with highly contrasting climates, topographies and cultures. It simply doesn't work.

That is the model we must replace in the coming years. Replace with one which fulfils the needs and aspirations of sentient human beings, not robots. Such a society will no longer pander to big business, the war machine and technocratic control system based in Brussels.

The new model will be essentially egalitarian and humanitarian. It will be founded on the principle of drastically closing the obscene earnings gap between 'rich' and 'poor'. It will recognise an essential equality between all occupants of this planet, and put into effect a resource management policy founded upon 'minimum harm' to human, animal and natural living environments, and maximum support for the health and welfare of all sentient life forms.

It will not, I say again, be a 'market economy' as we know it at present, but an economy 'as though people and the fabric of the planet mattered'. Money will lose its position as the totem around which everything else takes second place.

With reliance on globalisation and Big Pharma set aside, Europe, once again composed of many 'independent and interconnected countries', will develop a non-toxic health program which draws upon the deep wisdom of natural healing methods available to all cultures of Europe and the World. People will start coming alive, rather than dying.

The education programs of individual nations will centre around bringing out the innate creativity which exists in all young people. This resource will, in turn, help shape the new direction of society itself. Whereas at present, much of what is called 'education' is simply an exam machine. A factory conveyor belt supplying slaves for the corporate dominated and controlled 'job market'.

This is not education, it is indoctrination.

The emancipation of 'the spirit of man' will be central to the post EU era I envision. It will be recognised that this supreme human attribute, our spiritual power, has been deeply repressed. Repressed by an aggressive and regressive insistence upon money, prestige and power being the supreme goals of society.

Religions dependent upon dogma and the accumulation of wealth will have to take a back seat, as values associated with developing the true spirit potential of the individual will gain ever greater importance in a renaissance of post-EU independent nations.

Violence, crime and narcissistic self-interest, which have greatly increased under the jurisdiction of an out of touch centralised superstate and its associated warmongering governments, will become a thing of the past as our true human qualities re-emerge. Qualities directed towards the realisation of as yet barely awakened expressions of creativity, compassion and sense of oneness with fellow humans—and indeed with the great breadth of nature herself – of which mankind is a part.

Lastly, crude nationalism and xenophobic tendencies will lose their appeal as diverse countries link up to combine their socio-cultural strengths and common aspirations for liberation, emancipation and genuine evolution of the consciousness of the individual.

The political class, so deeply corrupted under the self-interested goals of phoney leadership, will fade away altogether, as 'people-led' initiatives gain ever greater influence at the local and regional level.

Eventually forming arts, cultural and administrative hubs that are firmly in touch with the needs of communities. The words 'European' and 'Union' will eventually mean something very much more real than the cruel facade which has been used to deceive the people of Europe for the past five decades.

We are the power of change. Our vision will become our reality. Not overnight, but imperceptibly, as conscious awareness steadily builds across the planet.

The depth and intensity of our desire for positive change determines the outcome. Have no doubt about that. Whereas to retreat from the challenge ensures remaining forever chained to the wheel of slavery. It's up to us.*

On the faultlines of change: local versus global

Virtually everything that conventional wisdom teaches about 'economics' is undergoing changes of an almost seismic nature at this time. Albeit mostly beneath the surface of superficial day-today activities.

The old model, which is still being forced along the ageing and unbending tracks of tunnel vision determinism, teaches that 'economic growth' is the be-all and end-all of

---

* See 'Changing Course for Life' new title 'Creative Solutions to a World in Crisis' for an in depth description of this vision.

planetary prosperity. Never mind that it is quite literally 'costing the Earth' and will require another five Earths if all seven billion citizens are to achieve the supposed goal of attaining a 'standard of living' equal to that of post-industrial countries like Northern Europe.

Yet, according to its advocates, an eternally expanding globalised economic market place remains the only valid prescription for this long-suffering planet. They still adulate notorious figureheads of the past, such as Adam Smith and John Maynard Keynes, neither of whose visions of a sustainable economic order have proved equal to the actual task at hand.

The best way to visualise the activity of a marketplace which deals in finite planetary resources as though they were infinite, is a man in a tree steadily sawing off the branch he is sitting on. And yes, he's three quarters of the way through that branch at the time of going to press...

But there is another paradigm pushing its way up through the morass of discarded steel and concrete which constitute the scrap-heap-earth economic order; and that is an altogether different baby, with its roots in preindustrial revolution practices where the land and its resources were regarded with respect and awe, and held to be essential to the health and well-being of all who engaged with them.

Here, manual dexterity and an inherited knowledge of good land husbandry were the hallmarks of sustainable living and the guarantee of good food on the table as well as a robust weatherproof home.

The simple values adopted by countryside communities were largely sacrosanct because they were closely associated with life and death, for the whole family. One lived close to the ground and got to know that ground intimately as a result. Mistreat it, and one blew one's life line to security and prosperity.

Stand these two models side by side and reflect on which is the more responsible template for the survival of planet Earth, its flora, fauna and human inhabitants.

Those who hold that the status quo still provides the solution for an expanding global population, should do a bit of serious homework. They should consider the fact that 40% of the World's best farmland has been rendered incapable of growing food, due to around 150 years of absolute exploitation of the soil by large scale monocultural farming practices and the profligate application of millions of tons of toxic pesticides and synthetic fertilisers; all of which deplete the life force of that most valuable of all resources: the top twelve centimetres of soil which all cultivated edible plants depend upon for their nourishment.

The true cost of industrial agriculture and the global market place it supplies is not reflected in the price one pays for one's food. That remains a hidden cost which governments and corporations keep firmly under wraps, lest the truth should emerge about the mining operations that are taking place under the pretext of 'efficient modern farming'.

In the UK, some 60 tons of topsoil per hectare are lost from arable land every year to the ruthless 'efficiency' of high-tech, soulless mining operations conducted by Big Pharma Agribusiness Plc. Bear in mind that it took millions of years for nature to build that topsoil. How could mankind have become so blindly profligate?

I have spent the last forty years nurturing back to life soils depleted by a reliance upon toxic substitutes to time-honoured natural soil building methods known to all true stewards of the land. In the process I found that a living soil produces living food, and that living food only retains its life-giving energies, but only when sold and consumed within the immediate proximity of the place of production. This is the secret of abundant health: in soil, plant, animal and man.

It stands in supreme contrast with the lifeless, denatured fake food which some 75% of the supermarket addicted population of Europe—and 98% of the USA—depend upon for their daily diets. So-called 'food', which has traveled an average of more than 7,000 kilometres before arriving on the neon lit plastic shelves of your nearest superstore. A starkly powerful symbol of factory-style mass production and the globalisation of the food chain.

The economy which emerges out of the ashes of the crumbling Keynesian model will bring us all back to earth, with a bump, I suspect. It will be one in which bartering and various forms of simplified exchange come to the fore, and it will be based on the exchange of real items of value, at the local and regional level. Not on the electronic, virtual reality money markets of today.

Emergent also, will be advanced renewable energy technologies that enable individuals and whole villages to go 'off-grid', thereby avoiding slavish reliance upon vast corporations. The same applies to materials for house building. Most will be drawn from natural resources like clay and straw, hemp, rammed earth and wood from sustainably managed forests.

In case readers should think I'm talking about some futuristic utopia, let it be known that models filling this description are already in operation all over the world. In the UK, alternative currencies operating under what are known as 'LETS Schemes', are gathering momentum. The Bristol Pound, which is supported by the mayor, operates in over 100 small community-oriented businesses in the city. The Lewes and Totnes Pounds have been part of community life for more than 20 years, and such creative alternatives to mainstream trading are springing up in London, Liverpool and many other towns and cities throughout Europe.

We are, by necessity, returning to our roots, and all those who can read the writing on the wall, should set their sights on getting re-earthed before the fault lines of change finally swallow up the outmoded and dysfunctional practices of yesteryear.

The democratic experiment is finished

We in the West have lived with this thing called 'democracy' for a good few centuries now. It has been an important experiment, but one which has, in the end, succeeded in swallowing its own tail rather than leading society to a better place. Now its time is up, and we have the task of putting something genuinely better in its place.

The most well-known definition of democracy—but by no means the first—is enshrined in the Gettysburg Address of November 1863. It proclaims democracy as 'government of the people, by the people, for the people' which—maybe for good reason—laid a strong emphasis on 'people'.

But here also lay its weakness; people (it turned out) had other ambitions that this form of self-rule was ill equipped to address.

Nor did they particularly want to be responsible for deciding and managing the intricacies of the experiment that they had signed up to. The majority, that is.

And it is this word 'majority' which encapsulates the failure of democracy, because, as some of us will have noticed, 'the majority' have never yet been possessed of the vision and wisdom necessary to move society towards a meritorious goal.

At best 'the majority' have created some form of social justice which was not around under the leadership of a sovereign (king/queen) unless such happened to have a social conscience. Democracy thus became akin to a personal insurance policy, in which one signed-up to the policy and paid the annual cover, via taxation. In return, one got a type of guarantee that one would have certain 'inalienable rights', backed by 'the law'. A law supposedly designed to support this form of self-rule, but in reality providing a cosy revenue absorbing niche for the same exploitive elitist element that had been around well before the democratic experiment came along.

As it turned out, what the majority actually wanted was based upon self-interest and not a vision of a better society for all. So give 'the majority' the right to decide upon whom they wish to run their country and the ones they actually elect will be those who have gone the most out of their way to claim 'to have their interests at heart'. The interests of the majority.

A society under the mantle of 'democracy' therefore never evolves. Instead it simply revolves around the wishes and the fears of the electorate. The wish to be 'looked after' and the fear of not being looked after. The majority simply elect a bunch of babysitters so that they can go out and play, leaving the actual responsibility for the shape and function of society to others, mostly those who enjoy flirting with the power that has been granted unto them.

The electorate then complain loudly when things get done by those in whom they entrusted power, but fail to live up to their fawning pre-election promises. It is a constantly repeating pattern which still shows no sign of abating. It is 'mob rule' in action: the undirected, unaware voice of a majority who readily succumb to the powers of the hidden persuaders.

The people, when this means a majority of the people, have never yet, throughout the course of history, been in possession of the wisdom and vision which are the necessary prerequisites of an evolving society. A society asked to raise its level of awareness, consciousness and responsibility.

The democratic experiment is thus an entirely inappropriate tool for getting out of—and going beyond— the mess we are currently in. It is simple naivety which is on display at demonstrations where placards are held up announcing that such and such 'is not democratic': 'TTIP is not democratic', 'the WTO is not democratic', 'tax avoidance is undemocratic' etc.

Over the years, democracy has formed itself around an unshakeable alliance with capitalism. Capitalism is generally held up as 'democracy in action', particularly in relation to 'the free market' as a self-adjusting silent voice of the people.

It is indeed in the marketplace that the majority have put their faith; and left those who claim to have mastered its intricacies to operate according to the nefarious rules of competition and greed that dominate the neo-liberal global economy which is the capitalist empire's crown jewels.

An economy where multinational corporate sweatshops in Third World countries can give the majority exactly what they want: 'cheap clothes' 'cheap food, 'cheap cars'. That my friends, is our famous democracy in action...and those who say "that isn't democracy" fail to realise that the majority voted in those who condone and execute these deeply exploitive policies. Voted in via 'election by majority' vote: the cracked cornerstone of the democracy experiment.

Not only this, but when challenged by someone touting the merits of communism, the answer comes "but communism isn't democratic" thus wittingly or unwittingly, holding up the flag of democracy as though it was a symbol of a free and progressive society.

Like religion and like the Mafia, democracy has provided a formula which offers protection for those who prescribe to a skewed system of control by the few. It puts a nice gloss on that which is, in reality, a sophisticated game of double deception.

A deception which has its roots in the electorate's abdication of control over its own destiny. Choosing instead to play victim to a system it helped put in place.

Today, eyes are slowly opening to what it is we have saddled ourselves with. Be it under the name of Conservative, Socialist, Liberal, Republican, Democrat or whatever—it makes not the slightest difference. They are simply entertaining variations of the same theme, and that theme remains mastered and controlled by a shadowy elite which quietly pulls all the main strings of power and will allow the game to be played strictly within its own terms—and no further So where do we go from here?

By we, I mean that smallish minority who are capable of rational thought informed by a bit of vision and wisdom.

This group cannot exert any serious authority upon the society around it, because—in a democracy—a small minority cannot form the majority necessary to becoming an elected administrative body. But at least we are not going to deny that, should 'a council of the wise' be at the helm of regional, national and global affairs, the world would be a different place. The value systems would be reversed. Instead of money, power and selfish self interest dominating the scene, we would have humane values, deep ethics and genuine justice as the main prerogatives, within an eclectic, multi-ethnic society.

There are still tribal societies that operate on such a system. They are called 'primitive' and are vindictively linked to a scary voodoo world of witch doctors and unruly shamans. Every attempt has been made to wipe them off the map, both physically and by our 'democratic' Western value system's high-minded judgmental view on this ancient, time tested form of 'leadership by the wise'.

As we once again find our true spiritual footing, our thoughts naturally turn back to this form of society by the wise, because it is an organic response to our deeper, actual and non-superficial needs.

No wonder the North American Indian tribes were wiped out or driven into special 'reserves' by their European conquerors; likewise the native South American tribes and the Aboriginals of Australia. The 'democracy' that supplanted them could have no truck with such deeply rooted and nature attuned cultures.

The capitalist free market needed to exploit their sacred territories and rip out the uranium, gold and all other precious metals which, while under the ground, informed the vibratory geography of their holy sites.

The supposed 'civilisation' which plundered the native territories, was largely a Judeo-Christian fabrication. One with a strongly Eurocentric bias and a penchant for grandeur and unashamed material wealth. Nothing of ancient tribal or pagan origins had any place in this great show of unabashed self-importance. And it is from this tradition that most people reading this book will probably have received their education—or more properly said: indoctrination.

Yet along with its pride and arrogance, there have been some idealistic ventures in various parts of the world into territories that bear some resemblance to 'leadership by the wise' and these belong to the category of 'benign dictatorships'. Fidel Castro of Cuba; Friedrich the Great of Prussia; Mustafa Kemal Atatürk of Turkey; the king of Bhutan, are some examples. Dictatorship is far less complicated than our form of democracy, but only if it is 'benign' can it be deemed genuinely superior.

A number of great spiritual leaders have filled this role of benevolent dictator during times of national crisis. Their followers, seeing that they possess the qualities that combine love and leadership, consequently feel happy to live under their guidance. Great leaders always encourage the best to come forth in mankind, bypassing power and self-prestige in favor of leading by example.

This form of 'leading by example' runs closer to universal spiritual principles of conscious leadership than anything democracy has, or can, ever come up with. When earthed and coupled with village level self-determination and a 'council of the wise', it probably constitutes the best role model we have to guide humanity through the crisis that is now upon us, and only likely to worsen. That is, until a majority of human beings finally recognise themselves as responsible entities, ultimately only answerable to a higher source of consciousness.

None the less, it is beholden for all of us who are both willing and able to see a bigger picture, to now give serious amounts of time and energy to thinking through the basic tenets to be put in place so as to bring about the world that will replace the present crumbling dystopia.

We must, as an imperative, lay the foundations of the life to come even before the present fiasco has reached its lowest point. That is the true meaning of taking responsibility for our destinies.

No time left—the dynamics of the new resistance

By all accounts time is speeding up and space-time is contracting. As we move further into the 21st century this phenomenon is almost palpable. Just where do the hours and days go?

Terence McKenna, the late psychedelics-inspired luminary, spoke of an imminent convergence of timelines that would bring about a 'singularity' event: the point where past, present and future become fused into the vibrant chords of the 'here and now'. Just what might such an event portend?

Time is a human invention, a tool for measuring the changing circadian paths of the planets, the phases of the moon, the passage of night and day. It is a useful device, but can easily become the opposite when relied upon too heavily. Indeed, the division of time into hours, minutes and seconds has mostly been used to delineate the financial value of the work day—a far cry from its cosmic origins.

McKenna's singularity event (which is not the same as the Transhumanist version) describes the condensing of all 'time' (past events) into an ever more energised and suspended state of 'presence'. For example, he speaks of the condensing of the last 64 years into just 12 months. A process that captures and passes through to us, the vibratory 'echo' of significant historical events that have taken place over the intervening decades.

As these spiralling time-lines pass ever closer to each other at ever shorter intervals, so it is that 'time' appears to speed up and we are moved ever closer to the 'simultaneity' event: an hourglass of tightly swirling energy whose vortex we ultimately pass through, emerging out on the 'other side'.

Now, you don't pass through a vortex and remain the same person you were when you went in! Such is the dynamic, that our vibratory levels resonate at a higher frequency during this passage and at a higher level of consciousness. It is what the Saddhus of Asia extol their disciples to achieve: the state of 'Be Here Now'.

Westerners may prefer to call this experience a 'rite of passage'. Those on this journey will get further support by dint of our planet's shifting into an alignment with the centre of our Galaxy. All this, you understand, is what I have gleaned (with added poetic licence) from the writings of others more fully versed in these matters than I. However, I find their discourses trigger an intuitive response which connects me up with thousands of others probably having similar experiences and similar observations. Are those of us who share such vibratory signals somehow emerging as a new power on this planet?

I believe we are. It is notable that our heightened perceptions are running in tandem with parallel 'scientific' lines of enquiry, such as the excitement generated among the scientific community by their probable discovery of what has been termed the 'Higgs Boson' (the God particle) at the particle collider centre near Zurich; the revealing of the manifestation of 'intelligence' within human cellular tissue in advanced biology circles and the first delineations of the invisible forces that bind the universe in the field of spiritual/quantum enquiry.

What this seems to mean is that we who go out into the world to confront the forces of destruction that are attempting to take control over our planet, are now being endowed with new powers to fulfil our task. Put another way, we are in an accelerating process of realisation of the potential which has always existed in each one of us to perform what one might term 'super-human' tasks.

And let's face it, the tasks we need to perform are super-human if we are to wrest back control over our destinies.

Those who stand behind the top-down control system and manipulate events with their occult and Masonic practices, are aware of the energy changes taking place at this time. They are trying to exploit them for their own ends.

Take a look at the 2012 London based Olympic Games; the opening and closing ceremonies exhibited a veritable coven of occult symbolism, unashamedly presented in big, brazen performances to wow the crowds. The perpetrators use such occasions to harvest both human and non-human energies for the realisation of their dark agendas. All the time keeping popular attention on the mundane and surface spectacle of 'the big show'.

Such techniques ensure that any manifestation of deeper truths will be fogged out by the sheer size and intensity of the gladiatorial spectacle. In the case of the London Olympics, billions demonstrated that they were only too pleased to show their submission to the 'greatest show on earth'.

However, the 'out of world' manipulators cannot themselves pass through the process of metamorphosis that we are experiencing, and this is their Achilles heel.

As we become more conscious and further imbued with higher dimensional awareness, the ambitions of the power-seeking elites become ever more naked. Their despotic actions being revealed for what they are, highlighted like ink spots on a white canvas. The heightened powers that we experience are the awakening of our own latent potentials.

For some this may prove a rather overwhelming experience, especially as it is accompanied by the rapid absorption of a lot of far-reaching information which will inevitably contradict previously held assumptions, such as those put about by the world's mainstream media.

To balance out this high voltage information intake it is increasingly important to become properly 'anchored'; our feet well and truly on the ground. Here, gardening, carpentry, bread making, food preparation and manual pursuits of all sorts—yes including the washing-up—should be performed on a regular basis as necessary counterparts to the often heady vibrational load that can otherwise overcome us.

This is the time to plot the practical sequence of events that will undermine humanity's oppressors and ultimately evict them from their pedestals of power. All this energy we are receiving must be turned into practical, pragmatic actions that lead to us wresting back control of our lives, as well as being used to support all planetary beings suffering under the cosh of a global dictatorship in the making.

Any residual elements of fear associated with taking such steps will be burned off once we come together in various groupings to build a web of resistance, and take on our oppressors.

Already, tens of thousands all over the world are orienting themselves into life situations that will support and be complementary to the new levels of awareness being acquired. I describe a situation manifesting itself as 'non-compliance' with the diktats of an increasingly authoritarian state. 'Non-compliance' in the face of ever more brazen attempts to make us conform to the demands of a corporate cabal and a despotic leadership fully intent upon the annihilation of our civil liberties and fundamental human rights.

All good resistance strategies integrate both the components of 'defence' and 'attack'. The defence of our fundamental needs and attack that will unseat those who would destroy them, are to go hand in hand in any campaign for an emancipated planet. The new energies and consciousness with which we are being endowed are specifically equipping us for this task. The cosmic timing is impeccable and the slave drivers have no weapons in their arsenal capable of suppressing the rising tide of universal consciousness that is the central ingredient of a deepening universal consciousness.

Our strategic planning for the battle in which we have no alternative other than to become engaged, demands concentration, creativity and courage. It is already in movement, and we must expect stiff resistance from those who deeply fear their coming fall from power.

All the symptoms are already at play. The almost daily introduction of new forms of oppression; ever more onerous surveillance techniques; unauthorised arrests; false flag dramas; internet interference; weather manipulations; the fomenting of new wars; genetic manipulation of the food chain and animal kingdom; the practice of mind control; depopulation via designer pandemics; banking heists; political and corporate despotism and much, much more... All tools in the relentless drive to achieve the long-term objectives of a New World Order and absolute control of all arteries of planetary life, tied into a vastly reduced world population.

Sinister it most certainly is. But we have allowed this situation to develop over decades through our passive acquiescence to each turning of the screw. And that is no longer possible.

Ultimately, true resistance is born out of the combined elements of a back-against-the-wall finality of the process of retreat, and the timely cosmic alignments that endow humanity with a greater capacity to confront and vanquish its oppressors.

That is exactly where we are today. The merging of convergent time lines has brought us to the front line. There can be no turning back. We each have specific roles to play in this drama and these will emerge as we commit ourselves to the cause. There can be no sitting on the fence any more. The fence itself is collapsing under the dead weight of decades of vacuous human intransigence. Words too. Use them carefully from now on, they carry more and more power. Power to build creative solutions and power to destroy.

All this, as the planet itself undergoes geological shifts and transformations of increasing magnitude. Let us remind ourselves that our Earth is a living being and is bound to show symptoms that reflect the predominant human condition. This is not to rule out cosmic influences; Earth is a place which reflects the inter-meshing of cosmic and human influences.

It is the lack of comprehension of this fact that has led to the dissonant dialogues on global warming and the overly simplistic conclusions of a tunnel vision-oriented science. Here we see how only a partial answer can come from a partial comprehension. Similar to the diagnosis of a Western medical doctor in comparison with that of an Ayurvedic, Chinese or homeopathic practitioner.

We are coming to see the connection between multiple elements and therefore are in an ever stronger position to take action in the process of healing our planet.

This is an urgent task indeed, and one that undoubtedly requires us to respect this powerful Mahatma Gandhi insight:

"Civilisation, in the real sense of the term, consists not in the multiplication, but in the deliberate and voluntary reduction of wants."

Here must we all go, for this is a profound truth that has been echoed down the centuries by the wisest minds. For us in the West, it is by pursuing an agenda of 'voluntary simplicity' that we can best offer a healing balm to planet Earth and to the overloaded mental and material complexities of our own lives.

Even as the Polar ice cap melts; the heartlands of the USA burn to dust; wars rip apart Middle Eastern valleys and mountain tops; earthquakes shatter communities and block vital supplies—our response should remain consistent and answer to the deeper underlying causative agents that lie behind all these events.

We must forge ahead with the building of life supporting 'Arks' even as we simultaneously confront the banking gangsters and their corporate accomplices. There is no time to lose. And anyway, time itself is undergoing this profound metamorphosis which is condensing all of history into a whirling vortex of cosmic cleansing and reordering.

A reordering so complete that it will ultimately leave us freed of karma and in a place where there is quite literally 'no time left'. That's where we're all headed, so drop off your old skin and face the rising wind with the spirit of the warrior who kindles a flame in the plexus and compassion in the heart. And be prepared to ride out the storm and to come to the aid of those who need your helping hand.

This journey is unprecedented; the possibilities infinite. It is we who hold the outcome in our hands. No one else.

Becoming Conscious

A great initiation called death

There's no point in pretending it's something not to think about. We do anyway, don't we? But it's how we think about it that matters—and how we feel about it, even more so.

Carlos Castaneda, author of The Teachings of Don Juan, rivets our attention on the ever imminent reality in proclaiming the Shaman's rule: that unless one can stand face to face with the unflinching reality of death— one is unsuited to the role of warrior traveler.

Now some might retort "We are not aspiring to be warriors anyway, so why make a big deal out of it?" OK, but let's not confuse the more standard war-like connotation of that word 'warrior' with its further meaning as: warrior traveler.

You see the 'traveler' factor is very significant; it means something that moves, that is not static. It suggests a continuing exploration, a voyage, change an unfolding event, doesn't it? Many reading this are no doubt warrior travelers in the making; brave explorers within the divine drama of life.

But many more might wish to be, yet feel a little fearful of the many unknowns that face the would-be initiate. I suggest that we all recognise this dilemma and share the insecurities and questions it raises within us.

So, just like any of life's innumerable hurdles, we can start by looking at 'passing' as a creative challenge. There is clearly an art to dying just as there is an art to living. The question is, what might that art be … and will we be lucky enough to have a generous and largely pain-free space of quietude in which to perform it? That would indeed be a blessing.

I'll have a stab at answering these rhetorical questions, but please bear in mind that they are my particular take on this—and I don't pretend to suggest otherwise. This is a flight of the intuitive led imagination.

If dying is an art, then the first thing is to recognise that it is 'art in progress', as it were.

We are talking about 'transition' are we not? We are talking about moving through different states of existence; different dimensions. And in order to make as smooth a transition as possible, we can benefit from preparing ourselves in certain ways.

All artists have to embrace the discipline of practising and developing their skills, otherwise their talents are wasted. So we too can benefit from some discipline as our prelude to the act of passing.

Thus the art of dying may be enhanced by arranging a few practice sessions before finding ourselves (our souls) on this journey—whether we like it or not.

I have explored the possible nature of this transition as an extension of the discipline known as Hatha Yoga, and have gradually come to sense what it could be like.

This comes through the widely practised discipline of 'complete relaxation' which is performed at the completion of the various stretches that comprise the majority of Hatha Yoga techniques. Many, I'm sure, will already know about this relaxation technique.

'Complete relaxation' is about letting go. So, I believe, is transitioning. Lying on one's back with arms out to the side, one lets all the stuff of daily life fall away to be pulled down to the centre of the Earth; using a type of downward gravity that applies itself to the abstract thought process.

These largely useless thoughts are then consumed by a fire at the Earth's core, and the pure energy, stripped of its burdensome weight, floats upwards into the cosmos. The trick to releasing this energy is to abandon one's self completely to Source; Divine, Supreme Creator—or whatever force one feels brought one into this cycle of existence in the first place. For it is that same force that will take us home.

While spread-eagled on one's back one gives one's self over to benign universal powers and requests to be cleansed and healed: to lose one's 'I-dentity'; the dispensing of ego. Letting all the 'I' centred thoughts fall away, until a deep calm and lightness of being prevails and a subtle sense of becoming spirit gradually takes over. One might then experience a subtle sense of floating upwards, just as the weight of the physical body falls away.

It is here, at this gentle point of separation between material physicality and spirit ether that we get something akin to a memory of transitioning into the vastness of the infinite. Infinite love. A dimension state named 'heaven' in the texts of old.

On the first part of this journey the presence of brilliant rays of light may become manifest. Soon those photons will be experienced as a state of being. Light as a state of being. Soul and light conjoined as one; expanding in intensity on the vibratory notes of a swelling symphonic resonance.

The speed of ascent may then quicken as 'spirit I' is pulled rapidly towards a magnetic point of great radiant power. It is here where a profound cleansing is initiated, causing our soul seed to merge into a great pool of highly energetic fecund plasma; freed of all the molecular earth-bound energies that were a requirement of dealing with third density worldly existence. It is here where the soul seed (what remains of 'us') is melded into the vibratory expression of Essence itself.

Essence, vibrating at such a high velocity that it forms an oasis of profound stillness. The omnipotent melding of the dual. That which encompasses both Alpha and Omega points as One. The One.

That is the culmination of the outward journey. And also the culmination of an inward journey.

The inward and outward journeys arrive at the same source point they started from.

From here is fired the ecstatic 'birthing cosmos' double spiral. The re-beginning. Blasting the seed of fresh awakening life back out into the next great unfolding cycle: a further phase of the adventure of 'our' purified spirit. Either re-experiencing life on Earth as the baby emerging from the womb of woman; or proceeding on another journey, guided by Source, to perform a role which gives further service to universal awakening.

As regards our individual journeys; well, they will be determined by our karma. Each journey is unique, yet in many other respects, similar. But the transition from 'material' life to 'spirit after-life' and onward into higher densities—or back to third density material existence once again—has one thing in common for all of us: its astounding mystery!

An intriguing part of this mystery surrounds the question: who decides if we return again to planet Earth?

It is my belief that we decide. But only if and when we have achieved (or maintained) a state of conscious awareness during the majority of our time on Earth.

Anyhow, a joyful embracing of 'the great mystery' is itself a vital factor in moving outward, onward and upward. In saying this, I'm not advocating a denial of true scientific exploration. When genuine and passionate, this complements our intuitive awareness.

Not so long ago, such a sense of mystery echoed out from the well-thumbed pages of little books of fairy stories. Our eager young minds were opened as were our eyes, by the sense of wonder and anticipation which these tales invoked in us. That sense of mystery needs to prevail throughout our lives and into our passing; in spite of the ultra-crude attempts being made to flatten, denigrate and ultimately destroy the living joy which is our birthright and cause to be.

After all, is it possible to observe sparkling water, swooping birds and gleaming forests—in fact any facet of the bounty of nature—without a sense of wonder?

Where are we if we can no longer rejoice at the miraculous emanations of the great cycle of life and death? Where are we if we cannot be overcome, from time to time, by the astounding wealth of diversity and mystery that underscores the unfathomable journey which we are all on.

Where are we if we see in all this simply the ordinary, the inert and the functional? Where are we if it all comes down to just some sort of routine mediocrity; some soulless daily ordeal?

As the epitaph on the tombstone in an English graveyard declares: "Here lies John Adams. The fact that he died does not guarantee that he lived".

And that's just it. To die well we have to live well. That means fully and generously; seizing every chance we have to fully utilise our potentiality, imagination and creative aspirations. Using them to bring justice to an unjust world. To boldly confront deceit with truth.

That is the prerogative attached to being 'human', and that which makes us proud of being human. A state we cannot accomplish when cut off from our fellow earthlings or when seeking solely to secure our own self-interests or narcissistic ambitions. That is a road which runs counter to our deepest callings.

It results in the fact that death becomes a much feared event. Feared because death most assuredly terminates the wilful cravings of the ego. Most surely shreds the puffed-up vanities of narcissism; and most surely confers upon its carrier further cycles of atonement, before 'the passing' is able to bring about a true freedom of spirit and an onward journey of joyous exaltation.

Yes, to die well—we must live well; in which we include giving others a leg-up on the road of life wherever possible, so that they may have the chance to shine and find the divine in themselves. Giving a lift to those who can benefit from our help, whatever their walk of life, whatever their failings or seeming faults. That is a fundamental expression of service to humanity which we are bound to put into action.

For in the end that person and we are unified in our struggle, sharing the same emotional pulls, needs and internal and external agonies and ecstasies.

Is there not one great pool of consciousness in which all we 'human' beings find shared commonality? And isn't it imperceptibly rising at this very time? Are not the walls of 'difference' steadily breaking down?

For, at the centre of this pool of consciousness, is the cyclic mysterious ferment which has no observable life or death, but just an ever expanding IS. And that is where we are heading at the completion of our temporal physical existence on planet Earth. And that is where we all came from 'once upon a time'.

That eternal, supreme and boundless state; at once all time and at once no time. This is what in store for us. Rejoice in this, a great initiation indeed!

Healing the psychic split which causes war

A World at war is the manifest outward projection of widespread inner human conflict.

A World where nations see other nations as 'enemies' reflects the external projection of unresolved internal fears.

A World where light and dark are conceived as irreconcilable opposites reflects an inner world torn asunder by rampant conflict.

It is inescapable: so long as we are at odds with ourselves, we are agents of external conflict. There cannot be 'peace on Earth' until there is peace of mind amongst Earthlings. That is an irrefutable truth which we do well to remind ourselves of.

As we grow into something approaching spiritual maturity, we start discovering and experiencing such truths at an accelerating rate. What's happening here is that we are making contact with sublime knowledge, and finding out that it has been with us all along, but that we weren't ready, or courageous enough, to integrate it on the emotional and psychic level of our daily lives.

But now we are—and this opens up a quite extraordinary vista of potential. Suddenly the world seems a different place. Our internal battleground of seemingly endless conflicts dissipates away into the background, and into the foreground comes a sense of our almost infinite capacity for integrating and unifying all seemingly disparate energies.

Yes, a great healing is underway here, and it is this same healing process which is the essential key to achieving the seemingly illusive goal of world peace.

Once we realise that we possess this remarkable power, we must use it. And here comes the moment when we also grasp that world peace is not going to happen just because we finally discovered our microcosmic version of it. Nor can we wait around until enough others have also acquired such qualities, so as to bring about the 100th monkey tipping-point of world change.

That, I'm afraid, would be an all too accommodating tea party at this point of history. The cucumber sandwiches and Earl Grey tea won't be magically appearing just yet, even if we ring repeatedly for Jeeves to set the table according to our wishes.

No my friends. Now we are faced by the true test. One in which we will either be revealed as fakes, who, after discovering our inner strength, chatted merrily away about how wonderful it is but then withdraw into the shadows immediately real action is required of us. Or, we will be revealed as those who seized the initiative to recapture the ground lost through years of indecisive uncertainty.

Here lies our sternest test. And although I used the future tense, this issue is not in the future, it is now. Right now.

Right now, even as you read, there is rising within a feeling of rightful indignation. Rightful indignation concerning the intervention of a lesser self which always tries to grab your attention at such critical times.

This indignation is an indispensable fire. A fire which guards against the capitulation of the life force and loss of self-integrity. Grab a hold of it—and don't let go until it has consumed you from head to toe, for only then will you be free to slowly release your grip.

Yes, the rules of the control game are tough to break out of; for they propagate division where there should be unity, and a fake form of unity where there should be division. They make night and day into irreconcilable opposites, when they are, of course, two parts of one whole. They hold up the 'pursuit of wealth' as the great unifier, when only the division and redistribution of wealth can bring about lasting unity.

'Us and them' remains the chief mantra of our society's authoritarian control system. It fuels the split, which has been the intention from the beginning, to keep divisiveness, fear and war at the forefront of daily life. For out of the ruins which result, the masters of control build up their empires and increase their leverage over the disenfranchised majority. The few reinforce their indoctrination of the many.

How can the many break out of this slavery?

There is but one way. One way which comes in two parts. Firstly, become conscious of the false divisions that play havoc with our deeper sensibilities—and heal them. Secondly, go forth bravely to play your part in helping to heal the wounds of this war-torn world. Take on roles of responsible leadership and help others gain a practical foothold on the ladder of conscious life.

Everything always comes in two parts, as a minimum. Every inhalation is followed by an exhalation. Every taking-in is followed by a giving-out. And that applies to our own taking from and giving back to that which sustains us.

Life is 'alive' due to the friction that exists between two complementary (yet opposite) energetic forces. Electricity is electricity due to the friction exerted by opposing positive and negative currents oscillating in immediate proximity with each other.

Without 'two' we cannot have 'one'. It is only when the intensity of friction produced by two energetic poles of attraction reach their zenith, that a state of oneness comes into being. No wonder the word 'enlightenment' is used to describe the state where the two fuse into oneness.

In third density existence this is largely a temporary condition. One which reverts back to its dual state as the zenith moment subsides. But returns to oneness once again on the next climactic upturn. And so on.

In quantum physics, which describes the fourth dimension in which everything is connected to everything, the form taken by this movement operating on the cosmic plain, is described as a 'standing wave'. Standing waves: constant peaks and troughs, oscillating with each other like beats of a musical score. Peak and trough waves, generating the very matter of life. Both at the minutest cellular level and at the vastest spectrum of the macrocosm.

Make peace with this duality, and you will find yourself in a place of great inner calm and purpose. Never go to war with that which is an innate gift of life.

Today, even within circles of the relatively aware, duality is often misconstrued as being responsible for a state of division, conflict and alienation. This is only true if and when duality is removed from its primal, higher dimensional role, and is placed in the three-dimensional setting in which every day modern society life operates today. In this setting it is deliberately made to look like a source of conflict.

Giving duality 'a bad name' is the role of social engineers. Those who are tasked with twisting the truth into its opposite and then making this distortion into the politically correct cornerstone of social conformity.

A classic example can be found in the current ubiquitous use of the expression 'you guys' when addressing a group of men and women. 'Guys' in US vernacular, once meant 'men'—like 'blokes' in UK vernacular. But now 'guys' covers both males and females, morphing them into one sexless unit. Or, simply making women into men, denigrating the innate sexuality of both.

This linguistic slippage is deliberate. The neutering of the sexes removes the innate male/female attraction of opposites which is at the essence of all life—rendering this dynamic meaningless, as in "we're all the same". The trouble is that we're not, and it is precisely our difference which both distinguishes and excites us. And excitement is a prerequisite for the manifestation of life energy.

'You guys' simply dilutes this power into some kind of insipid, denatured soup. Deflating our natural pride and distinctiveness in the process. It is a powerful tool in the dumbing down of human intelligence.

The true integration of seeming opposites does not dispense with these opposites (as 'you guys' does) but brings them into harmonious relationship, so that they no longer appear as agents of an internal war. This integration is the task we all have to perform in order to find our true place in the great cosmic order from which we originate.

It is the task we all have to face in overcoming the curse of war and the terrible price it exerts upon humanity – and the natural environment upon which humanity and all beings depend. War, whose deliberately incited presence hangs like a poisoned chalice over our divided planet, even as I write.

For I wish to remind my readers once again, war stems from subconscious, unaddressed and unresolved internal conflict. And so long as it remains unaddressed and unresolved, we will blame others for our own state of disharmony. We will say "It's them— let's destroy our enemy".

Fully accepting our natural duality heals the psychic split which otherwise drives mankind towards a permanent state of schizophrenia, paranoia and psychopathic delusion; the end result of which is the physical act of war itself.

We shouldn't be fooled by the fact that many succeed in wearing these destructive ailments relatively lightly; often even with a smile on their face! But this is a well disguised mask, worn due to a fear of exposing unresolved inner conflict.

The desire to conform to the social norm of the day is a powerful opiate for hiding the symptoms of disease. But they are there none the less, and often only just under the surface. The psychotic state of society, in which almost everything accepted as 'normal' is, in truth, highly abnormal— means that we all live in and amongst a kind of institutionalised insanity.

The maintenance of this socially engineered condition is overseen by the architects of control, whose sense of security rests on the condition that as few individuals as possible wake up and become healed, fully integrated human beings. A state which instantly blows the cover of both our external oppressors and the source of our own internal self-deception.

So there we have it. The path to truth is paved with hidden road blocks, the most important of which cannot be skirted around, but need consciously dismantling, brick by brick. And the deeper we delve the more sure we are to run into the road blocks which reflect a divided self.

But look, our brain has a left and a right hemisphere which are connected by a bridge 'the corpus callosum', and that bridge offers a big clue about creating unity out of polarity. Of discovering the unity within duality, and the fact that our intuitive and rational minds are entirely complementary.

There is nothing living which does not crackle with the electricity of duality. Even in a same sex relationship, male and female essence continues its dance, reflecting the different roles adopted by each partner.

We are all both masculine and feminine. Feminine and masculine. But the male genome normally predominates in man and the female in woman. However, this does not negate the reality that both are inherent in the genetic composition of both sexes.

Getting them into a state of dynamic balance within, is the imperative for a creative, fulfilling and joyous existence. One which takes us beyond division and violence which leads to war.

On the macrocosmic level this is Yin and Yang. Balance. Not through sublimation and negation of duality, but through embracing it as the indispensable motor of our self-development, and driving force for bringing to reality a world of enduring love and peace.

Seven stumbling blocks on the road to consciousness

The purpose of Life is to Live! But upon arrival on this Earth it quickly becomes apparent that this is not the agenda. Ninety-nine percent of what's going on here is not about enhancing human creative potential, but about suppressing it.

It's about stepping onto an invisible ladder whose rungs form the seemingly inviolable rules of a stagnant, pyramid-posturing status quo. A status quo which has almost nothing to do with growing, but a lot to do with decaying. With becoming a well-adapted slave in a world whose taskmasters are kings of a two-dimensional sub-reality.

That reality, as we have discussed elsewhere, consists of a monotonous fixation on the acquisition of power, money, prestige and pre-eminence. A world in which a quite deadly lack of awareness remains the prevailing condition; ruthlessly maintained by a small cabal in whose interests it is to keep things exactly as they are, lest some unguarded rebellion should dislodge them from their imperious, sterile thrones.

However, the life force is strong. It cannot and will not tolerate eternal repression. Wherever fissures appear in the status quo, it bubbles up and declares itself to be the messenger of truth. "This is our World. We are breaking free and shining a light on the path to be manifest."

So what is it that is still holding back so many from actually making that illumined path manifest?

Fear:

Breaking through the cosy similitudes of a largely routine, safe existence, takes courage and conviction. There is no 'easy way' to truth. But the thought of venturing into a deeper side of one's self—and of jumping into new paradigms of external involvement—often arouses a sense of fear.

Honest internal and external exploration brings things to the surface that many would rather leave buried and, as far as possible, forgotten.

Such embarkations into previously uncharted territories are, for many, an unsettling experience; one where our deeper intuition appears to be at odds with our mundane fixations. Where the inner call to be awake clashes with all too easily accepted patterns of day-to-day existence. Patterns whose 'successful' completion ironically, require that one remains largely asleep!

Fear can—and does—create the single largest block to the manifestation of our basic consciousness.

The manifestation of consciousness is not a passive affair, it demands taking action. "An action that speaks louder than words." And here's where the next level of inner, fear-based resistance kicks in and tries to hold us back from making a stand. Tries to prevent our involvement in positive acts of resistance in response to the further erosion of the planet's life support system. And to the further erosion of essential facets of daily life right in our own backyards.

Overcoming the hold which the fear factor exerts upon us is, I believe, the single greatest step we can make towards the emancipation of the true self and a rising consciousness. There are one hundred and one different ways of doing it, but recognition of the paralysis it causes in us is a major first step.

Low Self-confidence:
There are many amongst those longing for both internal and external change who fall at the first hurdle due to a seeming lack of self-confidence. A lack of self-esteem. But this need not be, for this sense of 'lack' is a trick played upon us by a wayward 'second self'. A little devil who has acquired entry into our subconscious and is lost if he is going to quit without a fight!

He's a cunning one all right, because he disguises himself as our actual thoughts; making us believe that 'we' can't do such and such—because 'we' are not capable—'we' are not good enough.. But it ain't the real we speaking, it's the little demon which Carlos Castaneda refers to as "a foreign installation". And yes, it is a foreign installation. And a devilishly clever little trickster to boot!

Try putting a proposal (to yourself) to do something for which you feel a great need, but have not as yet taken the step of actually putting into practice. Now, as soon as the foreign installation kicks in with "But I can't … it's really not possible…" you know it's that little Lucifer fellow. He's tricking you into believing that 'you' arrived at this prognosis, when actually he did. "But I can't…"

Yep—that's him!

Once you know this you're on your way. Once you disentangle your real self from that foreign installation— you have one foot on the path to the promised land. No 'buts'— unless you feel a positive urge to boot that little demon in the butt!

Laziness:
Yes, well, let's admit it, getting off one's 'butt' and getting going isn't the easiest for some people. But most forms of la-

ziness stem from being unmotivated and unwilling to make the effort to become motivated.

There are certain days when we all feel it; days when the energy seems to be drained out of us and nothing really comes to our rescue to kick the mood. But that form of 'enforced' lack of motivation can be in our best interests, as it may well stem from too many days of over-exertion without a break.

It's not the same as the kind of built-in lack of get up and go which afflicts millions, sometimes for long periods of their lives. This disease, and it is such, is more often than not associated with being 'too comfortable'. Too wrapped up in one's own self interested state of material well-being to ever consider doing something for the good of the greater whole.

This affliction is particularly prevalent amongst those who feel safest when operating in a club-like atmosphere where maintaining a public face of cheery conviviality acts as an insurance policy to protect against ever having to think and act 'outside the box'. To ever get truly serious about the dire nature of the predicaments faced by mankind and mankind's planet—and indeed one's own neglected soul.

For these beings, the only thing to jolt them out of their lethargy, is a disaster. And so, it is that millions will in fact face just such a disaster, as a form of karmic retribution for failing to make use of the gifts bestowed upon them.

This form of 'waking up as a last resort' is clearly to be avoided. Our World needs action in the here and now—and not years of inaction in never-never land.

Being Different:

Here's another barnacle-encrusted old anchor chain that's been holding back the evolution of large segments of often thoughtful individuals ... for far too long.

So it starts with worrying about what other people might think about one, especially if one is intending to embark upon something which fails to conform to the politically correct menu of the day. It's a form of paralysis which blocks any instinct to move away from 'herd mentality syndrome' with its rigid confirmation to what are considered 'acceptable' parameters of behaviour.

So powerful, for many, is the pull of trying to appear normal, that few openings exist for the true individual to ever emerge. What a tragic waste of human potential!

The prevalence of this condition is particularly well suited to the goals of the centralised control system. The one which sets the agenda of daily life on our planet. It plays into the hands of the top-down politics of persuasion through ensuring basic conformity with whatever the majority might be up to. Not daring to ever speak out against even the most foolhardy propositions and practices, lest one should appear 'different', is a disaster area of global proportions, especially in the face of ill-conceived and often abject acts of deception which we witness almost every day of our lives.

I've got news for those who suffer from this affliction: you're not going to be your own best friend in later life if you fail to make the effort to overcome your shyness now. Because either the frustration will build up to the point where sickness intervenes, or you accept becoming just another number amongst the robotic crowd. A crowd that operates without any true emotions ever breaking the surface.

That's an ugly choice to have in front of one. So why not break free today? Stop hiding your light under a bushel; step out and let it shine!

You'll be amazed at how much brighter everything becomes once one ceases trying to be like Mr, Mrs or Ms Normal...

Stuck in the Wrong Job:
This one is a major energy sucker, as anyone in this position surely realises. The inventor of the nine to five work day sure came up with a clever control mechanism for keeping mankind terminally preoccupied. Preoccupied with 'earning a living'— pretty much 24/7.

What is this? Shackled to a desk in a neon lit air-conditioned sterile office building with only a computer as work mate? Or maybe not quite as dull as that, but nevertheless, enforced and usually slavish routine day after day. A routine that ultimately only succeeds in bringing in more dosh to a business or corporation whose end product is just one of millions steadily destroying the health and welfare of planet Earth and most of her occupants. Get out of there – and fast!

Better to be on the street than in this kind of prison. Better (by far) to be working for yourself, not for someone who is only out to use you, prior to installing a robot a year or two down the road. The kind of robots that don't ask for wages. You know. They're even better than the ones that do, like you.

The typical nine to five job leaves no time for the type of deep reflection required to move forward into a state of conscious awareness. How could it—when 90% of one's energy is used up fighting to survive in the job market jungle. The rat race.

Our survival as human beings demands more than the monthly pay cheque. It demands that we are able to hear the voice of our true selves, and then turn its message to good effect in helping to shift the tide of history in a positive direction. Away from the neo-liberal capitalist money making machine and into something which calls forth a true power of awakening, sharing and social responsibility.

The Sceptical Intellectual:

"I can see that it won't work." Yes, sure you can! Because you made up your mind years ago that there's really no point in getting involved in any remotely idealistic initiative, since such initiatives are all doomed to failure at the hands of Mr Realism and his "I know best" crew.

There's something more than faintly fatalistic about our sceptical intellectual. Strange really, to build a pedestal for one's self and then set it in a concrete plinth, so as to be impervious to the swirling current of a life force which is capable of bringing 'a mountain to Mohamed' if that's what's really needed.

"Prove it". And when he says that, you know that everything which follows is something 'you' have to do—never him. For him, proof is actually never good enough anyway, because the mind which demands answers without ever trying to find them itself, is a sad and polluted vessel; badly in need of a full immersion detox. Yet many of these sorts of people are just the ones to become bankers, army corporals, political strategists, bureaucrats, professors and civil servants. They are the glue that holds together the status quo. Very reliable at carrying out their duties and ensuring that nothing too imaginative or spontaneous ever gets in amongst the automated cogs and wheels of the sanitised status quo.

The best cure for such individuals is to suffer an insufferable shock ... like falling in love.

Is it possible? Something that shakes them to their roots and causes a little volcano to erupt deep within. That which is capable of blowing away the densely packed layers which have caused a crust of cynicism to form over buried benign feelings of compassion, joy, creativity and yes, love. Something which turns on its head all the false pride of an over-indulged, obese ego.

Lack of Passion:
This is very bad news. Nothing, but nothing, truly meaningful comes into being without someone, somewhere, having a strong desire to bring to life their deepest needs. The manifestation of our inner powers is all about following through on that which inspires us. Inspires us to take action, to create meaningful change.

That should be the very definition of 'living' of 'being alive'. All the rest is shadow boxing with phantoms. And happy are these phantoms to be given so much unearned attention.

It is passion which created life in the first place. Passion is the precondition for all genuinely creative acts. It is the motor of universal movement. It is the dance of life!

Yet, for tens of millions of human souls it remains an almost entirely missing ingredient. And if, God forbid, it should ever rear its beautiful head, it is greeted with as much indifference as its recipient can possibly muster!

Come on! Sustained intent, fuelled as it is by passion, poses a massively intrusive threat on the control system's determination to keep the lid on human emancipation. It is the key without which we cannot unlock the door behind which we have for so long been imprisoned.

Look, I'm not talking about 'having a blast', going to a rave, or even getting worked up about something nasty going on in the neighbourhood. The architects of control have arranged all the outlets you will ever need to 'let off steam'; such sporadic outbursts of passion are well catered for.

No, I'm talking about a deeply sustained burning intent which simply will not die; once you've given it your recognition and grasped the implications of its transformative powers.

It's the reason I write. A deep need to share a vision of something. Something out of the ordinary. Sharing my thoughts and aspirations with you, dear reader. That's all part and parcel of this passion—which catches fire in those who are ready to burn.

That's it! And it all bubbles up from a place which is inseparable from Source. It is Source. Passion is 'the original energy'.

So how could one hope to Live Life without this primary force playing its fundamental role in everything one does. I can barely imagine. It's not possible. For whatever that thing is which happens between the time when we are born (on Earth) and the time we depart (from Earth)—it is not Life unless it is inspired by passion. It is a fake.

And, due to the fact that so many feel the need to fake their way through life, our World is starved of direction. There are too few helmsmen. It is largely directionless. The only forces to bring direction into this vacuum are the masters of control. The architects of fear. The instigators of war, oppression and violence.

Quite simply, it is the lack of 'we the people's' ability to sustain a passionate commitment to taking forward the callings of our destinies which is responsible for a global takeover by the pre-eminent despotic masters of oppression and control.

If we want to ensure that their days are numbered, and we surely do, we must dig deep. Yes, dig deep, always keeping victory firmly in our sights. The despots cannot endure a sustained barrage of many awakened souls. They fall away, exposed as the hollow cardboard shells which they really are. And we? We take the helm.

The Power of NO

When one feels and witnesses the crushing effect of the static status quo on all sentient elemental life forms, as well as on the great majority of human beings, one eventually reaches the point of saying "No, enough!"

Saying No comes before saying Yes, in the context of putting a brake on the slide into slavery currently besetting a great proportion of mankind. There comes a moment, in nearly everybody's life, when one makes a stand against some intolerable treatment which is being meted out by the forces of control and subversion.

Almost any incident could spark off the resistance: stifling and stultifying bureaucracy, the crazy behaviour of a neighbour, criminal bank charges, the dictatorial behaviour of the boss at work— any and all ways where the law is treated as a blunt instrument of repression. They all have a common source which centres around the deliberately oppressive, competitive structure built into our post-industrial westernised societies. One that crushes the humanity out of people. Although external in nature, the pressure builds and builds internally— until something gives—and one finally says "No! No more!"

That is a key moment and can turn the tide of one's life. However, the sense of liberation can be short-lived as further repressive elements are quick to occupy the void, unless one quickly fills one's self with something that goes beyond the purely personal; something that reaches out compassionately into the wider world.

Here is where the power of No is especially needed today. We have to recognise our innate connection with all mankind as well as with the natural environment; and we have to take a stand which reflects full-on resistance to that which is continuously undermining the quality of life of this planet. Indeed, its very survival.

Because without such determination, we will all sink into the cesspit of absolute submission to the deep state and its centralised control system which unceasingly seeks to dominate every artery of life on this planet.

For those who have gained enough awareness to recognise the deception, lies and villainy playing out their course right in our midst, there can be no excuse for not adopting a position of defiance and determination to play one's part in stopping the rot.

I know how easy it is to read hundreds of pieces like this and to get a temporary jolt each time, but still never actually take a stand; never really stand up to be counted. Never light that fire which pulls one out of one's set routine and plunges one into the battle.

It starts by saying No to the slippery slide into slavery. A slide which has been so well prepared to capture all who allow themselves the seeming luxury of ineptitude at a time of deep crisis.

But to take this stand, and to deliver, based on one's own sense of urgency to speak and act 'the truth' is an imperative which enriches our lives beyond recognition!

To know one has been caught in the tentacles of the superstate's ubiquitous web and to act on that knowledge, truly does lead on to individual emancipation. And, more importantly, it puts us in touch with fellow conscious beings who are already on the road which leads out of slavery and into taking full responsibility for their actions. It demonstrates a real determination to fully support that which nourishes, rather than continues to starve, our beleaguered Earth.

Here can be found the foundation of a new society. A steadily coalescing 'people's movement' which will collectively enable us to control our destinies and free this planet from its demonic overlords. Overlords who we have allowed to suck on our spontaneous creativity, passion and love, until it runs virtually dry.

That first big No leads directly to an even bigger Yes! To living out our true nature as conscious beings; defenders and guardians of this richly endowed place of beauty in which we find ourselves. You see, there is nowhere else to go with our lives. Those of us who 'understand' are in the last line of defence to bring an end to the despotic rape of all that which has value. Of everything sacred.

We are here for this purpose. It is our prime mission. Everything else is diversion or denial.

We are living in an apocalyptic and epoch-changing moment of evolution. But beware, for there are many voices telling us 'to just sit back and watch it happen'. And these are the pseudo-spiritual messengers of destruction; not the longed-for guides of higher emancipation that they claim to be. They are deceivers who play on a narcissistic tendency in the human race to only look out for one's own interests and try to ignore the plight of the greater life sphere.

No, we are, by now, wise enough to see through their devious ways and to reject the poisoned call for self-satisfied and self-centred passivity.

We are called upon to go forward with courage, cutting through the stupor of a sedated society; answering the call of our divine origins. A call to action. A call which starts with "No", yet transforms instantly into "Yes". Yes to joining in unity with all others who share a common commitment to truth, expressed in thought, word and deed.

Echo of the primitive

Between them, the upward aspiration of the Spirit and the pull of the Earth exert the two most fundamental influences on our lives. Strip away all the paraphernalia of modern life and the raw energies of these two forces take hold of us, opening up our latent powers.

What might appear to be two opposing forces turn out to be complementary dynamics sharing one original source.

To find our true equilibrium, it is necessary to get creative with these two dynamics. Let them speak to us, through us, so that we are re-imbued with the power that we have allowed to be stolen from us through centuries of denial. Denial, both by us and by those who set the trap which so great a portion of humankind has walked into.

These forces are dangerous. Dangerous, that is, for those who like to live their lives in a sterilised container. But they are equally dangerous for those who would like to keep mankind locked into such a prison. However, to those who continue to search fearlessly for the truth and struggle for its implementation, these forces are indispensable.

Certain native tribes and Shamans from the continents of America and Africa still hold this knowledge. Still live by it. Their lives are not cluttered by electronic wizardry, internet shopping and virtual reality. What you see in the wisdom-etched lines of their weathered faces is the expression of an absolute reality based upon decades of working with, and through, the aspiration of Spirit and the pull of the Earth.

What does that tell us about our lives?

It tells us that our sanitised 'face cream civilisation' is, by and large, an unmitigated disaster. A disaster which, if it will not fall apart of its own volition, needs to be taken apart piece by piece, so as to get back to a place where we can once again participate in the true current of life. Touch again the wisdom expressed in the ways of the native peoples.

In particular, it tells us that we need once again to find our place within nature and the elements and learn to work with them in the spirit of a loving, symbiotic engagement.

That is not as easy as it may sound. Making a life on the land is not for the faint-hearted. One would not see those lines on the native Indian faces and peasant farmers across the globe, if the life they eked out for themselves wasn't tough and often relentless.

But there are ways of living close to nature that do not involve being burdened by undue labor day in day out—and in fact most native peoples did not allow themselves to become 'tied to the land'—but celebrated the seasons and worked their territories in groups, communities and families—thus sharing both the hardships and the joys. That is the way we are to once again re-establish our working connection with nature in the years to come.

So it comes down to a rather basic question: how much do we really want to pare our lives down so as to be in touch with that which is real—as opposed to surreal?

Are we post-industrial Western bred and educated mortals actually able to even contemplate something so altogether different from what we know and see around us most days of our lives?

And if we can—what are the steps we would need to take to get to that other side?

I will try to answer that question. But first, let's consider what chances you would have of 'getting through' if you elect to make no change at all to your present circumstances. Here, I am assuming you are not already growing a reasonably high percentage of your own food; not having an independent source of pure water nor moving into the production of your own renewable energy— but are still living in a largely urban environment and primarily dependent upon the trappings of the corporate-run status quo.

If you are in this position, you are most vulnerable to being caught completely off-guard by a significant turn of events. And since there is increasing evidence of the likelihood of such a turn of events, I can only suggest that you would be wise to take seriously the predicament you find yourself in.

Bear in mind, that our goal is not just 'survival' but a deep re-engagement with the terrain of this planet. So that it becomes possible once again to experience the actual flow of Life, whose once joyful river has been dammed and muted beyond recognition. To re-experience that flow is only possible when, finally freed from the falsity of the superimposed and superficial matrix that presently directs almost all of our thoughts and actions, each day of our lives.

So what are the steps that those presently unprepared for what is to come should take?

Here comes the kicker: I am not going to say. Why not? Because you must work them out for yourself. They must be based on your free will to make the changes you know you need to make.

Telling you what to do only takes away the need for you to tell yourself—and at this late stage of crisis—it's your turn to take control of your destiny and not to follow someone else laying out the stepping stones to the other side.

You already know what to do—but you're putting it off. At my secondary school, after more than once putting off completing an assignment, the teacher told me to write 'procrastination is the thief of time' one hundred times. I never forgot that of course. Nor should you.

It's half past midnight now. Set the alarm—when it rings and you awaken—bring into your vision the weathered face of the Indian chief or squaw, and let it remind you of the ascent of the Spirit and the pull of the Earth. The upward thrust of aspiration and the downward pull of gravity; the powers that fuel the drum-driven tribal dance; that catalyse a tingling sense of ecstasy, expectancy—about where you need to be and what you have to do to get there. Then do it.

Epilogue:

Dialogue between a Master A and his Pupil B:

B: The Universe, or what is referred to as 'space', seems to be a kind of ethereal void, populated here and there by stars, planets, occasional meteors, comets and such like.

A: The Universe seems like a vast and mysterious place, but when you consider that it is contained within a dew drop or a human cell, it becomes less distant. In fact, it becomes very immediate. I refer, of course, to the microcosmic condensation of the macrocosm.

What is 'space'? It is not what it seems. The word does not describe the reality. It seems void because you are only using your five senses to analyse it. There is no 'space', the area referred to is full of energy. An energy field. But you don't recognise that which you can't experience with your five senses.

B: What other sense do we possess, other than that which recognises reality through touch, sight, taste, smell and sound?

A: We have our perception and intuition; these are receptors that pick up vibrational messages due to the absolute interconnectivity of all matter and energy. When you connect up with the source of all that is, you find that you are part of it, not distant from it. You cannot observe or experience it dispassionately— from a distance—because you yourself are part of the composition.

B: But rational observation forms the basis of all science, it enables us to understand the nature and structure of things, including the Universe. We want to understand how and what life is.

A: Such curiosity is a perfectly acceptable condition in mankind, but it arrives at the wrong answers; unless man feels himself to be part of that which he observes. Not only this, but recognises that he affects that which he focuses upon. Both intentionally and unintentionally.

B: How is this achieved?

A: One cannot say 'how' it is achieved, unless one is prepared to come at it from the opposite dimension and perception from that which one is accustomed to, in one's experience of everyday life.

B: Oh?

A: What we experience in our typical daily lives is that which operates, almost exclusively, within the realm of the five senses. Take sight: Visible light—what we 'see'—constitutes less than 0.5% of what is actually 'out there' in our Universe. Or 'in here' within our microcosmic and internal Universe. So we cannot understand, within the scientific discipline which belongs to the Newtonian school of thought, how and what life is, if we only rely upon our five senses to reach our conclusion. There is a missing dimension.

B: What holds us back from being able to experience this missing dimension?

A: Almost everything which forms the experience of what we call life, here on Earth. We operate within a three-dimensional framework which has become so institutionalised that we take it to be the sum total of everything that is. Whereas actually, it constitutes something quite alien and divorced from the true state of existence: that which we experience in the fourth dimension and beyond.

B: Tell me more about the fourth dimension and beyond...

A: You already know something about this. When you

fall asleep and dream, you are entering this dimension, subconsciously. When you get an 'inkling' about something— and then find that this inkling turned out to be true—you are also touching the fourth dimension. The problem is that, most of the time, you dismiss these experiences as being irrelevant to the tasks and needs to which you address yourself. Those tasks which form the daily diet of a materialistically aligned world. That superficial repetitive pattern which forms the central point of focus of life on earth at this time. That which broadly operates within what we call 'the status quo'.

B: I want to understand what this 'other dimension' is and how to have greater access to it. I do get these 'inklings' from time to time, but never really questioned where they come from.

A: All right. Intellectually, you can already get closer to the higher dimensions by using something of what (well focused) three-dimensional thinking has already been able to ascertain, concerning further dimensions.

Take that chair you're sitting on. It appears to be hard, doesn't it? But actually, when seen/experienced from the higher dimensional state, it is not. It is just a mass of whirling atoms, clustering together in such a way as to provoke the sense of shape and form we call a chair. If we understand correctly from science what atoms are, we would not describe them as 'hard'. Simply as 'energy'. Mutable energy.

Now, look at me, or look at yourself. We too, seen from the higher dimension, are also a whirling mass of energetic particles (called atoms). The only difference between us and the chair, is that we are imbued with a whole host of sentient, sensitive attributes which operate on a vibrational wave length tuned to a different (higher) frequency than that of the chair.

The fourth dimension and beyond, is actually our true home— where we come from. And in it, we exist as spirit energy. This spirit experiences life as a quantum event.

Everything interconnected with everything, everywhere, at all times. This quantum state is our true reality, and everything else is a falsehood.

B: A falsehood?

A: Yes, because in our true state we are at one with all creation. Which means at one with our Creator. The Divine Source of all that Is. Whereas, in a purely five sense, three-dimensional state of existence, we do not allow ourselves access to the vibrational waves of higher awareness that constitute the true universal state of reality. The 99.5% of existence we think of as 'beyond the realms of possibility'.

B: Is this 'lack of connection' the cause of our seemingly endless problems, here on Earth? Are we really living in such a tiny match box and imagining we are having a universal experience?

A: Essentially, yes. We experience most of our lives as something completely divorced from what Life actually Is. This has not come about by chance. It is a design which has been imposed upon mankind by a force whose motivation is alien to the will of the Creator, yet which vampires energy from creation. However, since we are gifted with powers that originate with our Creator, but have largely failed to apply them, we are complicit in the problem. We possess all that is needed to return life on Earth to its true state of creative resonance, but fail to do so.

We have instead, allowed ourselves to be won round by an alien force and its accompanying false agenda: its deception. So, as we awaken to our true reality, we must use the creative, imaginative powers with which we are richly endowed, to dismiss the three-dimensional impostor. The imposer of the three-dimensional deception—that we have confused with reality. The task of mankind is to rediscover and re-establish its connection to the source of all life.

B: Are we making any progress in that direction?

A: It is called 'waking-up'. This is an apt expression, as it suggests coming back from a state of unproductive dormancy. Universal energies, whose origins are the higher dimensions, are manifesting strongly on planet Earth at this time. The pace is quickening. The attempt to block that quickening pace and its accompanying awakening, is equally manifesting itself, increasingly obliquely. As a result, people are experiencing a critical confluence of disparate forces. The feeling, for many, is of being pulled apart; a type of dying.

The man and woman emerging out of this storm will be closer to their true state of being. Much closer. They will understand that they embody both sides of the disparate energy mix now manifesting. The alien and the true state.

They will recognise that both the creator and the destroyer exist within, and that each individual has the power of 'free will' to choose which to nourish into fullness. They will discover that they are—and always have been—in possession of higher instinctual and intuitive energies. Energies which, when properly directed, make it possible to avoid returning to a repetition of past errors.

They will realise that the source of their power is not their own. Does not belong to them, but is an inherited gift, a seed, whose origins rest with their Creator. Thus, rather than puff themselves up with false pride, they will honour the source from which their divine powers emanate. The life to come, here on earth and beyond, will be uniquely directed towards building upon the fruits of this deepening recognition.

In this way God and Man will be reunited—to put it better— will rediscover their unity. Their oneness. And the quantum Universe, with open arms, will welcome back the profusion of its presently disconnected and alienated parts, and thus become whole.

At that moment, the dance of all joyous dances will manifest throughout. And the purpose of Life will be revealed.

THE END